I Never Promised You a Rose Garden

www.**transworldbooks**.co.uk

Also by John Crace

Baby Alarm: A Neurotic's Guide to Fatherhood
Vertigo: One Football Fan's Fear of Success
Harry's Games: Inside the Mind of Harry Redknapp
Brideshead Abbreviated: The Digested Read of the
Twentieth Century
The Digested Twenty-first Century

I Never Promised You a Rose Garden

A short guide to modern politics, the Coalition and the general election

John Crace

BANTAM PRESS

LONDON • TORONTO • SYDNEY • AUCKLAND • JOHANNESBURG

TRANSWORLD PUBLISHERS
61–63 Uxbridge Road, London W5 5SA
A Random House Group Company
www.transworldbooks.co.uk

First published in Great Britain
in 2014 by Bantam Press
an imprint of Transworld Publishers

A CIP catalogue record for this book
is available from the British Library.

ISBN 9780593074381

Addresses for Random House Group Ltd companies outside the UK
can be found at: www.randomhouse.co.uk
The Random House Group Ltd Reg. No. 954009

The Random House Group Limited supports the Forest Stewardship Council®
(FSC®), the leading international forest-certification organisation. Our books
carrying the FSC label are printed on FSC®-certified paper. FSC is the
only forest-certification scheme supported by the leading environmental
organisations, including Greenpeace. Our paper procurement policy
can be found at www.randomhouse.co.uk/environment

Typeset in 11/14.5pt Sabon by Falcon Oast Graphic Art Ltd.
Printed and bound in Great Britain by
CPI Group (UK) Ltd, Croydon, CR0 4YY.

2 4 6 8 10 9 7 5 3 1

For Simon and Olivia

Contents

Acknowledgements

I Never Promised You a Rose Garden was commissioned well before I became the *Guardian*'s parliamentary sketch-writer. It is a job for which Simon Hoggart set the gold standard for more than twenty years until his death in January this year and one which I am honoured to have been given. I hope Simon would have enjoyed this book.

My thanks are first due to Susanna Wadeson at Transworld, for coming up with the idea and for being such an inspiring and steadying hand. I couldn't have wished for a better editor and therapist. Thanks also to Brenda Updegraff, copy-editor extraordinaire with a better grasp of grammar than I will ever have, to Kate Samano, Claire Ward, Sally Wray and Kate Green at Transworld, to my agent and frequent partner in disappointment at White Hart Lane, Matthew Hamilton at Aitken Alexander, and to Nicola Jennings for the stunning jacket artwork.

If the next paragraph reads like a list of the great and the good at the *Guardian*, it is because that is precisely what it is. A huge number of people have backed me, both before I started working in parliament with their support for the Westminster Digested column in *G2*, and since I began at the

House of Commons. Without their knowledge and help I would have been lost and the book would have turned out very differently. Thanks then to Alan Rusbridger, Michael White, Patrick Wintour, Nick Watt, Andrew Sparrow, Rowena Mason, Rajeev Syal, Flora MacQueen, Paul Johnson, Martin Kettle, Polly Toynbee, Rafael Behr, Jonny Freedland, Larry Elliott, Phillip Inman, Steve Bell, Will Woodward, Polly Curtis, Dan Sabbagh, Mark Oliver, Ewen MacAskill, Severin Carrell, Hugh Muir, Esther Addley, Sarah Hewitt, Clare Margetson, Emily Wilson, Malik Meer, Tim Lusher, Patrick Barkham, Kira Cochrane, Suzie Worroll, Simon Hattenstone and Catherine Bennett, aka the real SamCam.

Thanks also to my fellow parliamentary sketchers, Quentin Letts, Ann Treneman, Donald MacIntyre and Michael Deacon, for their warmth, encouragement, inside knowledge and laughter. I feel privileged to have been admitted to their club. Thanks also to Rob Hutton of Bloomberg for letting me steal his jokes and not making me feel I am the loudest person in the office, to John Sutherland for his lunches, friendship and literary criticism, and to the many others at Westminster who have also been generous with their welcome, time, wisdom and sense of fun. Special thanks to John Humphrys for reading the book in first draft and for giving such a wonderful jacket quote.

I haven't been easy to live with as I finished writing the book and got used to wearing a suit to work for the first time in fifty-seven years; so no thanks to Tottenham Hotspur Football Club for making my life even more stressful. On the plus side, I did have the love and support of many friends and my family; in particular, my fab wife, Jill, my two wonderful if rather too opinionated children, Anna and Robbie, and Herbert Hound. Without them, everything is just noise.

Chapter 1

2 + 2 = 5

SHORTLY AFTER THE GENERAL ELECTION OF MAY 2010, DURING the talks to form a coalition government, David Cameron, the leader of the Conservative party, and the Liberal Democrat leader, Nick Clegg, had a conversation. History will record it as an agreement to put aside the old party politics by the introduction of a Fixed-term Parliament Act that would prevent a prime minister from calling a snap general election and ensure future governments had a full five years to implement their policy programmes. The actual conversation is likely to have been a little more nuanced than that:

Clegg: I don't trust you.
Cameron: How can you say that?
Clegg: Most coalitions barely last a year. How do I know you're not just going to dump me?
Cameron: The thought had never occurred to me . . .
Clegg: Not even if the opinion polls suggested you would get an outright majority in a year's time?
Cameron: I give you my word . . .
Clegg: You do realize the country is in an economic mess and

that the government is likely to be hugely unpopular for at least three or four years? If not longer . . .

Cameron: And?

Clegg: And if I persuaded my Lib Dem colleagues to vote against the government on a key issue we could force another general election? And in another hung parliament we might just form a coalition with Labour?

Cameron: You wouldn't dare . . .

Clegg: Try me.

Cameron: No one would ever trust you again . . .

Clegg: They don't anyway.

Cameron: So what do you suggest?

Clegg: A fixed-term parliament. That way we're both locked in and neither of us will have one of the shortest political careers on record.

The Fixed-term Parliaments Act became law in September 2011. For the first time in Britain's history, the date of the next general election became universal knowledge. Labour, Plaid Cymru and the Scottish Nationalists tried to introduce an amendment limiting the fixed term to four years, but the Conservatives and the Liberal Democrats outvoted them and five years it was. Barring either the House of Commons passing a no-confidence vote in the government – and given the Coalition's majority this would require the government effectively to admit, 'You know what? We have been a bit rubbish' – or for two-thirds of all MPs to demand an early election – about as likely as them asking for their expenses to be re-audited, just in case they had over-claimed – then the next election would be held on 7 May 2015.

Under the previous rules, the government had been free to

call a general election at any time during the course of a five-year parliament. In practice, the only governments that delayed calling an election until they were statutorily obliged to do so were those who knew they were dead ducks and were just hanging on for a miracle – a spontaneous eruption of billions of tonnes of oil in the Thames estuary would be handy – and to get the most out of the ministerial limos. John Major knew the game was up long before the 1997 election: he had already resigned once as leader of the Conservatives in 1995, after being overheard referring to several of his Cabinet colleagues as bastards following a TV interview.

The power to call an early election at any time was a huge advantage for a government, allowing the prime minister to select the date that opinion polls suggested would be most advantageous. Even now, Gordon Brown must be kicking himself for not calling an election in October 2007. He had finally taken over from Tony Blair in June of that year. All the opinion polls suggested Labour would win an election with a reduced majority. But Brown bottled it.

You can understand why. Becoming prime minister had been Gordon Brown's driving obsession for years and he believed that Blair had reneged on several earlier deals to step down and let him take over. Having finally got his hands on the job he had always wanted, was he really prepared to risk everything on a snap election? What if the polls were wrong – they had been in the past – and he were to lose? Then he'd be no more than a footnote in history. The laughing stock of his nemesis, Blair. The man who was handed the keys to Number 10 without the need to win an election and was then rejected by the public when he did call one. Better to wait until the opinion polls picked up just a little . . . Except they never did.

The financial collapse followed soon after, the economy went into recession and Brown's days were numbered.

It's possible that David Cameron might have given up the massive benefit of being able to call a general election at a time that suited him as an act of fair-minded altruism. If so, then he would be the first prime minister in history to decide to level the political playing field in order to give his opponents a better chance. It's unlikely that Cameron sat in his office at Number 10 feeling overwhelmed by the existential crisis of his good fortune: 'I've had too many advantages already in life. It's just not right I should have any more. It's time to give that nice Ed Miliband a break.'

Cameron agreed to a fixed-term parliament because the Lib Dems demanded it as part of a coalition agreement and at the time it wasn't a deal-breaker for the Conservatives. Better to get the chance of power on a fixed-term contract than to risk missing out completely. That's how the political process rolls. Sometimes laws get passed for the good of the whole country, sometimes they get made mainly for the benefit of the people inside Westminster. Some of the knock-on effects of this constitutional reform could be predicted, if not quantified. Each parliament has lasted just under four years on average since the end of the Second World War: a five-year term gives voters fewer opportunities to re-elect or change a government. Whether the loss of some democratic accountability is compensated for by the stability of the new system is still anyone's guess.

There have also been a number of less expected consequences from the Fixed-term Parliaments Act. When the opposition faced the possibility of an election at any time, it needed to be able to present credible and coherent policies of its own. Labour has been under no pressure to do that: why go through all the effort of creating detailed proposals – which the government will pick holes in – for situations that will almost certainly have changed a few years down the line when the general election comes round? Far better to argue your own position in vague generalities while putting the government under the microscope. Which is mostly the game Labour has played in opposition. Even the party's own insiders still aren't entirely sure what the One Nation slogan, launched at Labour's 2012 party conference, really meant. Luckily, it doesn't matter that much, since it seems to have been reduced to ever fainter echoes.

One of the arguments used in favour of a fixed-term parliament was that it would allow the government to plan a full five-year legislative programme without worrying that important Bills would have to be dropped because of an early election. It hasn't quite turned out like that. All the Coalition's big – and difficult – legislation on deficit reduction and reform of schools and the NHS took place in the first three and a half years of the parliament. Thereafter things have gone rather quiet, because the Coalition doesn't want to upset the punters before an election. The general rule of government is to get the pain in early and be Mr Nice Guy – aka do not very much apart from the odd budget giveaway – before an election. The only moderately tricky piece of legislation to be negotiated in the final year was the HS2 Bill for the construction of a high-speed rail link between London and Birmingham. Even then its third reading was scheduled for a time comfortably after the May 2015 election. This year, next year, sometime, never . . .

The feeling that backbench MPs were left twiddling their thumbs was not lost on the opposition. MPs are known for being generous in awarding themselves long holidays – recess, they call it – but in 2014 they gave themselves even more holidays than usual. For once, though, accusations of wholesale slacking-off were wide of the mark. Most opposition MPs would have welcomed more activity. There was just nothing for them to do. If the government hadn't run out of ideas, it had certainly run out of legislation to put before parliament.

There's a little-known exchange that takes place in the House of Commons at about 10.30 every Thursday morning in which the leader of the House is asked by the shadow leader of the House what business the government has timetabled in the coming months. Normally it's a fairly anodyne session, but for a while in early 2014 it became one of the highlights of the week. The Conservative leader of the House was Andrew Lansley, whose sacking as health minister was almost a mercy act. Lansley is a tortured soul who moves so slowly it's as if he is hoping time will overtake him and transport him back to a more congenial era. The late nineteenth century. His opposite number was Angela Eagle, an altogether sharper politician.

Each week Eagle would taunt Lansley that the government had nothing to do and he would reply that the reason there was so little to do was because the Coalition had been extraordinarily efficient in expediting its legislation. Not even Lansley could look convinced by that. His nadir came in the final head-to-head before the Easter break.

'Perhaps he can now confirm that prorogation [the ending of the parliamentary session] will be at least a week, or even two weeks, early due to the government's chronic lack of business?' Eagle asked.

Lansley rose wearily. 'I am surprised at the honourable lady's argument that we are not busy. We are busy,' he replied. 'As it happens, when we return from recess, we have a busy two days.'

Lansley's own state of profound futility was so visible even his own party regarded him as fair game. 'Why are the government so frightened of giving Members of Parliament a decent time to debate the HS2 Bill?' enquired Tory back-bencher Cheryl Gillan. Lansley insisted he had given it a lot of thought and had allocated more than enough extra time. 'An hour,' said Gillan.

Lansley's expression made it clear he felt this was a huge concession to his social schedule. The speaker couldn't resist going in for the kill. 'I say gently to the leader of the House that, in extending the Monday sitting by an hour, I feel sure that he was taking pity on the chair and did not want the chair to be occupied beyond eleven o'clock. For my part, I would be quite happy to sit in the chair until at least three or four in the morning.' Lansley looked horrified.

Lansley was just the fall guy, though, the politician who shouldered the burden of government inertia. It wasn't his fault. That the government had so little to do was a direct consequence of the five-year Fixed-term Parliaments Act. Election campaigns used to last only a matter of weeks; a couple of months at most. Now they last more than a year.

Chapter 2

Should I Stay or Should I Go?

THERE'S OFTEN A POINT IN THE LIFESPAN OF A PARLIAMENT when the government knows the game is up: that no matter what it does it has no chance of winning the next election. Sometimes it comes after two or three years; on a few, rare, occasions it's reached on the very day after they've just won the previous election.

John Major's Conservatives experienced that moment of revelation in 1992. Their surprise election win that year had been more of a vote against Labour than an endorsement of the Tories: indeed, up until the moment Neil Kinnock, the Labour leader, yelled, 'We're all right! We're all right!' on stage at a political rally in Sheffield, many Conservatives had already resigned themselves to the inevitable. Kinnock's Bono impressions – 'Every time I clap my hands, I lose another vote' – were a wake-up call. The electorate might have been all right, but the Labour leader wasn't. Kinnock's efforts to appear as the new, engaged, populist face of Labour had backfired embarrassingly.

Lightning wasn't going to strike twice. The Tories' narrow 21-seat majority couldn't survive another five years: they had been in power since 1979 and the public were bored with them. Sitting in Number 10 on the day after the 1992 general election, Major knew he was on borrowed time. The country's apathy and disillusionment with the Tories was only ever going to increase over the next five years and all he could do was try to limit the worst of the damage. It was a thankless task as his government lurched from one crisis to another: first Black Wednesday, in which the Treasury lost £3 billion in a day trying to keep the pound in the European Exchange Rate Mechanism, then a succession of sex and money sleaze stories involving Tory politicians, along with ongoing rows within the party over Britain's membership of the European Union. Come the 1997 election, it's possible that not even John Major voted for the Conservatives.

Labour might have had much the same feeling in 2005. Most of the goodwill that the party had accumulated going into their 1997 landslide victory had long since dissipated. Their majority had been cut from 160 to 66: even though the economy appeared still to be OK, disenchantment had set in. Core Labour supporters believed the party had failed to deliver on many of its promises and – more importantly – that they had been misled over the government's decision to go to war with Iraq in 2003. The less committed Labour voters were just becoming apathetic. Close up, many Labour politicians had begun to look just as self-serving and back-biting as their Tory counterparts had done. Another five years of this and Labour would be done for.

No one understood this better than the Labour prime minister, Tony Blair. Following the death of the party's leader John Smith in 1994, Blair and Gordon Brown had had dinner together in Granita, a restaurant in Islington, during which many insiders believe a deal was reached to stitch up the leadership of the Labour party for the foreseeable future. If Brown didn't challenge Blair's candidacy, then Blair would step aside some years down the line and let Brown have a go. The exact details of the conversation have long been a matter of contention. Until now:

Blair: Very good of you to join me, Gordon.

Brown: I thought it was you that was joining me . . .

Blair: Would you like a glass of wine? No? The angostura bitters? A splendid choice. Anything on the menu that you would especially like?

Brown: I think I'll have the leadership of the Labour party . . .

Blair: It's off.

Brown: That's not fair . . .

Blair: New Labour has to move with the times. A certain amount of greed is good. Thing is, Gordon, ya know, the voters find you a bit scary. So we don't want to put them off, do we?

Brown: What are you saying exactly?

Blair: The guys think Labour stands the best chance with me as leader. And I have to say, I agree. But you will get your opportunity . . .

Brown: When?

Blair: Oh, I don't know, Gordon. Do stop going on so. Just try and enjoy being chancellor for a bit. You will get your turn as prime minister one day, I promise.

Brown: When?

Blair: Oh look! There's the waiter. So what will you have? I can recommend the sea bass . . .

Brown: I will give you two elections, Tony. Just two. After that, you bugger off and make your fortune somewhere else. Do you hear?

Blair: This stuffed squid is heavenly. To die for . . .

Brown: Two terms. No more. I want your word on that.

Blair: Alastair! Fancy you turning up . . .

Whether a deal had really been done and whether the Labour party would automatically have accepted Brown as its leader once Blair stepped down is conjecture; what isn't is that Brown felt a deal had been made and that the leadership would be his by right. Wind forward nine years to 2003. Gordon Brown was still chancellor; Blair had won two elections and was in his second term of office as prime minister, showing no sign of going anywhere. In his 2010 autobiography, *The Third Man*, Peter Mandelson, one of New Labour's more slippery architects, recorded that Brown and Blair were virtually on non-speaking terms by 2003 – primarily over Blair's refusal to step down: non-speaking, that is, apart from a series of volcanic rows late in the year. Mandelson has never been the most reliable of witnesses, so the conversation could have gone like this:

Brown: You promised you would go . . .

Blair: Didn't. I had my fingers crossed. So there.

Brown: I've always thought you were untrustworthy. And now the public think you are too. Just go.

Blair: Sometimes one must travel the road less travelled, Gordon. Nothing could be simpler than for me to walk away and let you be prime minister. Indeed, in my weaker moments there's nothing I would like more than to just put my feet up. But that's not what God wants and it's not what the country wants. I am here to serve. So you must stand and wait . . .

Brown: I've had enough of this . . .

Blair: Well, I haven't. What bit of 'I'm Not Going Anywhere' don't you get? I love it at Number 10. Cherie loves it at Number 10. Did you ever really think I'd chuck all this in for you? I've got my legacy to think of. Another election win and I become the first Labour leader to win three successive elections.

History was duly made, with Blair securing a third victory in 2005 with a further reduced majority, largely because the voters thought the Conservatives were still a shambles, with a leader, Michael Howard, who had been no more popular than the previous incumbents, William Hague and Iain Duncan Smith. But even as the last votes were counted, Blair knew his time was up. The public disliked and mistrusted him and no one believed in the New Labour project any more. Labour had run out of ideas, big or small. Government had been reduced to getting through day-to-day crises with as little damage as possible – something that was becoming increasingly difficult as the Labour back benches were filling up with discontented MPs who had either been overlooked or shafted by their leader. Blair had almost as many enemies in his own ranks as he had among the Tories.

In 2006, Tom Watson, a junior defence minister, met with several other Labour MPs at a curry house in Wolverhampton to plan a move to depose Blair as leader. Days later Watson resigned as minister and delivered a letter, also signed by ten other rebel MPs, to Downing Street calling on Blair to resign. Gordon Brown claimed he had nothing to do with the attempted coup and said the letter was 'ill-advised', though it was later revealed that Watson had visited Brown at his Aberdeenshire home the day before he delivered the letter. Watson claimed he had just happened to be passing by and wanted to pay his respects to Brown's baby son and that the letter was never mentioned. Even he didn't sound as if he believed that story. As with all other challenges to his leadership, Blair faced this one down, but he must have known his days were numbered. The main thing now was for him to consider the timing of his exit. Too soon and it would look as if he had merely been hanging on to win a third term; too late and he would just appear self-interested and spiteful. So he hung on for another year before calling Brown in 2007:

Blair: You win. I'm off.
Brown: What?
Blair: I'm out of here. Finito.
Brown: Just like that . . . ?
Blair: I've outgrown this job, Gordon. There's nothing left to do here. Everything's fucking up and the country hates us. Where's the gratitude, I ask you. After all I've done. Still, one has to be humble in these situations, so I'm moving on to bigger and better things. I've got peace to bring to the Middle East and my Blair Foundation to run.
Brown: Let me get this straight. Having taken all the credit as prime minister for ten years, you're going to bugger off when the party is at its least popular and leave me to sort out the mess?
Blair: Don't be so negative, Gordon. You've always wanted to be prime minister and now you've got your chance. Never say I don't keep my promises.

Not for the first time, Blair's self-preservation instincts were spot on. Whether by luck or judgement, he got out just in time. Within months, the global banking system was in crisis and the economy was heading for recession. And Brown, the chancellor who in 1999 had promised the country 'an end to boom-and-bust economics', was left to cope as prime minister with the fallout from the worst economic meltdown for over a century. It didn't help that voters perceived his manner to be awkward and defensive. But even if he had been as smooth and slick as Blair in the New Labour heyday, the situation would have been unsalvageable. Come the 2010 election, Labour would have to go. A Conservative victory should have been a mere formality.

During his time as prime minister, Tony Blair saw four Tory party leaders come and go. John Major stepped down straight after the 1997 election, William Hague went after the 2001 election, while Iain Duncan Smith didn't even make it through a parliament to contest the 2005 election. The honour fell instead to Michael Howard, who immediately announced he would step down after the Conservatives lost that election.

Of the four, only Hague could count himself as un-fortunate. At another time in his party's history, when the Tories weren't so universally disliked, he might have been a good leader. Hague has a sharp political brain and something almost approaching charisma. His mistake was to allow him-self to be put forward as leader when his party had no chance of winning an election. He was only thirty-six in 1997, and had he been prepared to bide his time for another ten years he could have been leader as the party's fortunes began to recover. But few politicians ever pass up the opportunity to take a top job when it's offered: most know that careers in Westminster can be all too short and the chance may not come around again; the rest have such big egos they believe they can be the ones who achieve the impossible.

Duncan Smith and Howard were more like sacrificial lambs. Neither had the personality or sharpness to convince either their MPs or the country that the Conservatives were a credible opposition, and their appointment had more than a hint of a *Beyond the Fringe* sketch:

Tories: We're looking for someone to make a futile gesture.
Duncan Smith: I will, sir.
Tories: Sorry? Who are you?
Duncan Smith: Iain Duncan Smith, sir.
Tories: Are you one person or two?
Duncan Smith: Just the one, sir.
Tories: Jolly good. Now look here, Duncan. The enemy are dug in over there and we need someone who is prepared to attack them on foot in broad daylight. I won't beat about the bush. It's going to be bloody. Bloody bloody. But someone has to do it and that person is you. Your country will remember you.
Duncan Smith: Thank you, sir.
Prolonged machine-gun fire.
Tories: We're looking for someone to make a futile gesture.
Howard: I will, sir.

If Labour party members had been allowed to vote in the Tory leadership contest, Duncan Smith and Howard would have romped home in a landslide. Whatever else Labour had to worry about between 2001 and 2005 – principally an unpopular war in Iraq and splits in its own ranks – the Tories weren't an issue. The choice of Duncan Smith and Howard suggested a degree of pragmatic resignation among the Conservatives. As long as the Tories couldn't win an election there was no point wasting their best ammunition. Better to keep the quality players fresh on the subs' bench and let two of the older, reasonably competent squad members have their futile swan song on the front bench.

The contest for the 2005 Conservative leadership election eventually came down to a two-horse race between David Davis, an experienced politician from the right of the party, and David Cameron, a relative newcomer from the left of the party, who had only been elected to parliament in 2001. For a while Davis was the front-runner, but a poor speech at the autumn party conference saw him slip in the ratings and Cameron got the job. His attractions were clear. He had no past and was therefore untainted by the failures and embarrassments of the Tories throughout much of the 1990s. His more liberal conservatism was in vogue: old-style, hard-line Thatcherism was popular only in remote outposts of the Rotary Club. Tories in 2005 had to look as if they cared. Cameron ticked all these boxes. What's more, he had an attractive wife, a young family, he had listened to pop songs on the radio – well, he said he had – and could sometimes be seen relaxing without a tie. This was about as common touch as any Tory politician had ever got.

The problem was that as the 2010 election grew ever nearer and the economic situation became bleaker by the day, it became more and more obvious that Cameron wasn't particularly in touch. Nor was he the Conservative's Tony Blair, as many had hoped. Cameron was a posh boy who had gone to Eton, moved seamlessly on to Oxford University, where he had been a member of the all-male, public-school Bullingdon Club – in which getting drunk, making sexist jokes, trashing restaurants and making fun of foreigners was a tradition – before joining the Tory party as a researcher. Apart from a five-year stint in PR for London-based Carlton Television, he had never had a job outside politics. No one could be entirely sure if he had ever left the Home Counties.

Nor did it help that Cameron had chosen the godfather to one of his children, a man with an almost identical background, to be his shadow chancellor. George Osborne had gone to St Paul's rather than Eton and had never had a proper job outside Westminster, but otherwise his CV also read Oxford, the Bullingdon Club and the Tory party. As a team, it wasn't so much that they lacked gravitas as that they had little to offer. They were two men who seemed to have grown up immune to the demands and complications of everyday life and had effortlessly moved into positions they considered their birthright. That judgement might have been harsh, but it was the way it looked to a lot of people, especially the ones who were losing their jobs and having their standards of living squeezed as the country slipped into recession.

As Labour ummed and ah-ed about how best to prop up the failing banks and scrambled for a viable economic policy for dealing with record levels of government debt, Cameron and Osborne didn't have any practical solutions of their own bar blaming the government for having got the country into this mess – overlooking the fact that the Tories had failed to spot the impending financial crash every bit as much as Labour had. Indeed, prior to the crash Tory economic policy was in many ways identical to Labour's. Though with a few small extra tax-break promises thrown in.

The remedies that both Labour and the Tories proposed after the crash were equally quite similar: cut government spending to reduce the level of debt. Both sides promised nothing but pain for the country for the foreseeable future; the only point of difference was how much government spending should be cut and how much pain inflicted.

Here Cameron and Osborne found themselves with an image problem. Whether their policies of bigger cuts and greater pain were more economically sensible became a secondary issue as people in many parts of the country suspected that whatever pain was inflicted would have less personal effect on the Tory leaders than Labour's policies would have on its Cabinet:

Cameron: We're all going to have to tighten our belts.
Osborne: Tell me about it. I've already cut back the cleaner's hours.
Cameron: Good man. I've axed one of my foreign holidays. We're going to go to Cornwall for a week in the summer instead. Could you do the same?
Osborne: I can't cancel the skiing trip, Dave. It's all paid for and the family would go mad.
Cameron: Fair enough, then. Just try not to get photographed on the slopes and do make sure you travel EasyJet.
Osborne: If only more people were prepared to make these

sorts of sacrifices in their everyday lives, then the country would soon pull through.

Unfair, maybe. But the idea of a growing disconnection between politicians in Westminster and the people they represented was taking a stronger hold. And as the election approached, with both Labour and Tories looking equally toxic, many voters began – for almost the first time – to wonder if either of the main parties had the answers to the country's problems.

Chapter 3

Hallelujah

BRITISH GENERAL ELECTIONS HAVE TRADITIONALLY BEEN A STORY of two-party politics. Initially, the battleground was between the Liberals and the Conservatives, but with the growth of the Labour party after the First World War, the Liberals fell into a rapid decline and every general election since the 1930s has, to all intents and purposes, been a contest to decide whether the Conservatives or Labour would form a government.

Not that the electorate had no other choices. A Liberal or – since the Liberal party merged with the Social Democrats in 1988 – Liberal Democrat candidate still remained on the ballot sheet in most constituencies and a few were even elected to parliament. Scotland and Ireland had their own nationalist parties – the SNP and Plaid Cymru – who won a handful of seats in their own countries. The Green party returned its first MP in 2010 when Caroline Lucas won the election in her Brighton constituency. The UK Independence Party (of which more, much more, later) put up plenty of candidates in recent years with nothing to show for it, while the far right – the British National Party – and far left – the Socialist Workers Party – had the same success (none) with fewer candidates. In the two Bootle by-elections of 1990, the Monster Raving Loony party attracted more votes than the Social Democrats in the first one and more than the rump of the old Liberal party in the second, but still no seat in Westminster. Some might call that a shame.

Though many supporters of these minority parties – especially those that were more primarily focused on a single interest – passionately believed in their cause, their votes were essentially protest votes. They were votes cast in the certain knowledge that their chosen party had absolutely no chance of forming the government, or even being the main party of the opposition. As much as being votes for something, they were also sending a big 'Not Interested' message to the Tories and Labour. One that said, 'You know what? I've watched both of you in action and you're so hopeless that I can't bring myself to vote for you.'

There are other forms of protest vote. Some people spoil their ballot paper by scrawling on it instead of marking their choice with an X. This at least has the benefit of being a vote that has to be counted, though since it gets lumped in with those who messed up their ballot paper through not really understanding why they were there or how the ballot worked, it's a form of protest that can be misinterpreted by the main parties and put down to dimness on the part of the voters. The same can be said for another type of protest: not bothering to vote at all, which has become an increasingly attractive option for many. In the last half of the twentieth century, the turnout for the general election was never less than 70 per cent; during the twenty-first century it has slipped to around 65 per cent. It is just possible that a large percentage of the country weren't aware there was an election going on, but much more likely that the electorate was becoming disaffected.

More to the point, the two main parties don't particularly care whether someone doesn't vote or spoils their ballot paper. They say they do, because that's the mature response and a sign of a healthy democracy, but, at a very basic, practical level, they don't. Elections are a simple numbers game in UK politics: under the first-past-the-post system, the candidate who gets the largest numbers of votes in his or her constituency is elected to Westminster. So if a party can't persuade you to cast your vote in its favour, it would much rather you stayed at home or spoilt your ballot than put your X in a rival's box.

Voting for a party other than the Conservatives or Labour is an active form of political engagement. It shows you care about the way the country is governed and that your vote could potentially be won by either of the main parties if they came up with some sensible policies. And yet – there is no way of getting round this – it is still very much a protest vote: an active signal that while you respect the processes of government, you are resigned to the fact that the people who occupy the key roles in those institutions aren't really up to the job. This may be a pragmatic truth, but it also gives immense freedom to those politicians in the small parties who are never going to be in a position of power.

One of the best things about being a Lib Dem before the 2010 election was that no one ever really hated you. You weren't important enough to hate. You could always be on the right side of any argument in the certain knowledge that you would never, ever be held to account in any practical sense. Writing a political manifesto was as much like writing a birthday-present wish-list as a considered commitment to action:

> We want to see an end to party politics. There is too much hatred in the world. We want a system where everyone gets on with one another and loves each other. We want a fairer world where everyone has a really interesting job and never gets ill. We want a world where everyone pays a bit more tax, but only if they really want to. If they don't, then that's OK too. We want a greener, more sustainable world in which polar bears and cockapoos can get along together. We want more sunshine and less rain, though obviously not in a way that promotes global warming. We want to teach the world to sing . . .

Who wouldn't want any of that? Who cared if it was totally impractical? Who cared if it was unaffordable? No one. Going through a Lib Dem election manifesto with a calculator and a red pen looking for inconsistencies was a category error. A Lib Dem manifesto was never meant to be a serious legal document. Everyone understood they were just a list of nice, fluffy things that might exist in an ideal world and there was no need to examine them too deeply because there was no chance of the Lib Dems getting anywhere near a position in which they might be expected to put their idealism into practice.

The Lib Dems were the party for those who wanted a better life but had no expectation of ever getting one. The deal was this: the Tories or Labour got to sit in the seats of real power, the fifty or so Lib Dems got to occupy the moral high ground. That's the way it was, and prior to 2010 that's the way most people imagined it would stay. The situation almost no one expected was that the voters would one day have so little faith in both the two main parties that the Lib Dems might hold the balance of power. It might not even have happened in 2010, but for one big miscalculation by Brown and Cameron.

In September 1960, a young, good-looking J. F. Kennedy squared up to a stubbly, pasty-faced Richard Nixon who had just come out of hospital for the first ever televised presidential debate. The political analysts scored the debate as a draw, but the TV viewers saw it differently: a clear win for JFK. Nixon wised up for the next three debates by shaving and slapping on the slap, but the damage was done. The TV audiences for the last two debates were far smaller than for the first and the public perception of Nixon as Tricky Dicky never really shifted. Before the debates JFK had been narrowly trailing in the polls; his TV appearance was a key tipping point in him going on to win the White House.

The Americans didn't bother with televised debates for the next three presidential elections, but since 1976 they have been an ever-present feature of the campaign. Where America leads, the UK generally follows, but British politicians found the calls for a leaders' debate all too resistible. The debates were too 'presidential', they said. They focused too much on individuals: British politics was about policies, not personalities. As if. The main issue was that elections were hard enough work for the leaders without giving your opponents an opening. The debates were just too unpredictable: they were elephant traps into which a leader could unwittingly fall. So why make extra trouble for yourself when you can just say no?

By 2010, though, the clamour for greater transparency and accountability in politics made it more difficult for both Labour and the Tories to put off a televised debate any longer. Refusing to have one when the country was in the middle of an ongoing economic crisis would have looked as if the leaders had something to hide, as if they were actively trying to avoid appearing together live before the country. Just as importantly, David Cameron perceived he might have something to gain from a debate. He was more shiny and media-friendly than Brown and he might win over some undecided voters. With the public and Cameron clamouring for a debate, Brown had no choice but to agree.

The leaders began their preparations and made their contingencies. The lessons from all the American TV debates had been studied and learned. Both sides knew their weaknesses. Brown could appear surly and defensive; Cameron could come across smug and superficial. Each party gave its leader hours of intensive media training so that all the bases were covered. Except they weren't.

No one had really factored in Nick Clegg and the Liberal Democrats. The presidential debates had almost exclusively been between just the Republican and the Democratic candidates, and British electoral campaigns had always been run with a similar bi-partisan focus. The Lib Dems and the other small parties weren't exactly ignored; rather they were treated as endearing pets that you could snuggle up to and stroke when the Tories and Labour got a bit boring. But not something you would ever take particularly seriously. Forming governments was something left to the two big boys.

The presence of Nick Clegg alongside David Cameron and Gordon Brown in the televised debates changed everything. For almost the first time, the media gave a leader of a third party equal standing with those of the two main parties. The subliminal message this sent out was that maybe it wasn't such a waste of time to vote for the Lib Dems after all. Maybe Nick Clegg and the Lib Dems really did have as much to offer as the Tories and Labour.

The televised debates looked rather like this:

Brown (*leaning forward awkwardly, while trying to make himself appear friendly*): These are tough times for Britain. And tough times call for a tough leader. I have shown I can be that tough leader. I haven't shied away from the difficult decisions nor will I do so in the future. When I was chancellor of the exchequer, I promised there would be no return to boom-or-bust economics.

Cameron (*sweating heavily*): The prime minister calls himself tough and yet he has only brought the country to its knees. Why stop at a double-dip recession when you can aim for a triple-dip? Where is his ambition, his vision, for the country?

Clegg (*blinking in the lights, yet beatific*): The way things are is not the way things have to be. Don't let them tell you that the only choice is between two old parties who have been playing pass the parcel with your government for ages. Give real change a chance . . .

Brown (*confused*): Who is this bloke?

Cameron: Buggered if I know, old boy. I thought he was a member of the technical staff.

Clegg: When I have doubts, I turn to the words of the great prophet Paulo Coelho. Tell your heart that the fear of suffering is worse than the suffering itself. When you find your path, you must not be afraid. You need to have sufficient courage to make mistakes. Disappointment, defeat and despair are the tools God uses to show us the way . . .

There are the first stirrings of a spiritual awakening in the audience. Brown and Cameron begin visibly to panic.

Brown's adviser (*talking into Brown's hidden ear-piece loudly enough for everyone to hear*): Calm down. Everything's fine. Try to stop hyperventilating. (*Brown takes several deep breaths.*) That's better. Now smile . . . (*Brown grins maniacally.*) Not that much! You're scaring everyone. (*Brown has several attempts at adjusting his expression into something vaguely normal and unthreatening.*) Just a bit less severe, Gordon. That'll do. Now say something that will go down well with Middle England.

Brown (*whispering into his jacket mike*): How about I mention that stupid old bigot from Rochdale?

Brown's adviser: Perhaps not . . . But reassuring everyone you're not planning to let every foreigner stay in the country should go down well.

Brown: I promise you here and now that I will personally make sure that anyone who is not allowed to stay in this country will be removed.

Cameron: So we have your word on this?

Brown: Of course. I will personally escort every single illegal immigrant back to Dover and make sure they get on the ferry back to France.

Brown's adviser: Oh fuck. Why do I bother?

Cameron (*trying to be sincere*): I have met a black man.

Gasps of 'He's met a black man' from everyone.

Cameron: A black man from Plymouth, no less. A black man who was serving me a pasty . . . (*he wipes away an imaginary tear*) . . . and this black man said to me that there are far too many other black men in Britain, and that if we continue to allow hundreds of thousands of other black men and Eastern European benefits cheats to come into this country willy-nilly, then life won't be much fun for the other black men of Plymouth.

Clegg (*holding out his arms*): Behold the futility of two-party politics. Consider the people of the valleys. Just as there are good Welsh people and not-so-good Welsh people, so there are good foreigners and not-so-good foreigners.

Cameron: I agree with Nick.

Brown: So do I.

Cameron: I was first . . .

Brown: No, you weren't . . .

Clegg: I have a dream. A dream where politicians stop arguing among themselves. A dream where politicians tell the truth and keep their promises. Except about university tuition fees or any other policy they never anticipated being held to account over. A dream where I can say to the people of Britain, 'People of Britain, I know these are difficult times, but together you can make the hard choices and conquer austerity.'

Cameron (*rapt, falling to his knees*): I agree with Nick . . .

Brown (*considerably less rapt, but reluctantly falling to his knees*): I agree with him more than you . . .

Audience: Rejoice! The Messiah is among us!

Clegg won the first debate at a canter and the second by a neck. Brown and Cameron came back strongly in the last one, but by then it was too late. Neither had really worked out how to deal with Clegg on television: their only two methods seemed to be either to ignore him or to patronize him. Both made them look bad and pushed them into a corner where they were forced to say they agreed with him. Clegg didn't really need to say or do anything very much. Not being Cameron or Brown was enough. Many voters looked at Cameron and Brown getting hot and sweaty and instinctively thought, 'Nah. I'll have the other one.' Within hours of the first televised debate, Clegg was being openly talked of in some quarters as 'the saviour of British politics'. He tried to laugh it off; but not too much. Being the saviour of British politics was quite a handy thing to be in the last couple of weeks of a general election campaign.

Chapter 4

Let's Stick Together

AFTER THE FINAL VOTES HAD BEEN COUNTED IN THE 2010 election, no party had won the required 326 seats to give it an overall majority. The Conservatives held 307 seats, Labour 258 and the Liberal Democrats 57: either one party would have to form a minority government whose legislation could only be got through parliament if all the others didn't gang up to block it, or there would be a coalition.

The situation wasn't unprecedented: there had been a hung parliament in February 1974 in which Labour ruled as a minority government after the Conservatives and the Liberals were unable to form a coalition, before calling another election in October of the same year in which they won a slender overall majority of three. But it was significantly different. Back in 1974 there was less chance of forming a meaningful coalition that could survive a full parliament, as the Liberals held only 14 seats.

There was also a feeling that the political landscape had changed. Many British politicians had always been a bit sniffy about coalitions, regarding them as a rather inferior form of government. Something that may be OK for mainland European countries – such as Italy, which so often lurched from one barely functioning administration to the next – but not something compatible with one of the world's oldest democracies. Now, though, while some commentators scratched their heads and declared it was hard to interpret what the electorate had really said, the voters had actually spoken quite loudly and clearly. And the message was that they didn't much like any of the parties and didn't want to give any of them too much power.

For Labour this didn't come as any surprise. Indeed, given the state of the country's finances and the general disenchant-ment with the previous Labour government, there was some satisfaction to be had in the result having been as close as it was and in the fact that Labour hadn't been wiped out as the Conservatives had been in 1997. The possibility of forming a coalition came as an unexpected and welcome lifeline for Labour. For the Conservatives – and David Cameron in particular – the result was borderline disastrous. Being the largest party in Westminster was no consolation. If the Tories couldn't win an overall majority when the Labour party was on its knees, then when could it? The Tory grandees and party donors were not at all pleased with their returns from the election and, if the situation were not partially redeemed, it wouldn't be long before Cameron was quietly removed. For Cameron, then, a coalition was a necessity. So both parties were ready to trade.

As were the Lib Dems. They might not have predicted the heightened levels of Cleggmania, but they had done the maths before the election and concluded there was a genuine possibility of them holding the balance of power. There was a world of difference, though, between the theory of being prepared to do a deal and the practicalities of getting one done. All parties were in uncharted water; there were no maps or guidelines telling them what to do and in what order and who could expect to get what. Everything was up in the air and they had to make it up as they went along.

With the Lib Dems clearly in the role of kingmaker, attention turned towards Nick Clegg. Though his party had actually won five fewer seats than when Charles Kennedy had been leader at the 2005 election, Clegg's status was far higher than his predecessor's had ever been. He was good-looking – which always helps: not even his closest friends would ever have described Charles Kennedy as being attractive. He wasn't Cameron or Brown, which was another huge plus. Most of all, though, he was untainted with the grubbiness of tribal politics. He had been painted as a man of integrity. A man who understood the worldliness of politics, but who could also rise above that world. It was a picture that Clegg was more than happy to go along with. If people wanted to project their own desires, fantasies and ideologies on to him, then let them. Look what it did for Chance the Gardener in the 1979 film *Being There*.

It had been those on the left who had been loudest in promoting Clegg's virtues before the election. That was partly because even its traditional, core supporters were finding it difficult to see the Labour government as anything other than a dead duck, but partly also because the Lib Dems' manifesto appeared to be a great deal more radical than Labour's. It wasn't a watered-down version of the Tory manifesto, as Labour's looked. It promised to create a more equal tax system in which the rich would pay more; it made a commitment to green energy; it wanted to reform the electoral system; and it said it would not implement the

proposed rise in tuition fees for university students from
£3,000 to £9,000 per year – all things which many Labour
supporters would have quite liked to have seen their own
party promising.

So when Clegg announced on Friday, 7 May, the day after
the election, that 'it was in the interests of fairness and
democracy that the Conservatives should have the first go at
forming a government', many people didn't read too much
into it. This was Clegg doing what a Clegg should do. Acting
with principle and integrity in letting the Tories, as the party
that had won the greatest number of seats, make the first
move. The conversation that Cameron and Clegg had at this
point was widely assumed to be:

Cameron: We need to do a deal if I am to be prime minister.
Clegg: What did you have in mind?
Cameron: I haven't given it a lot of thought. What do you
want?
Clegg: Be nicer to immigrants . . .
Cameron: What?
Clegg: No increase in tuition fees . . .
Cameron: You're kidding!
Clegg: Fairer taxation and electoral reform and . . .
Cameron: And? You've already asked the impossible!
Clegg: Several posts in the Cabinet.
Cameron: I can't do that.
Clegg: Then we don't have a deal.

That's certainly the way it seemed as if the conversation
had gone, as the noises coming out from both parties the
following day was that the talks, while amicable, had

reached an impasse and that the Lib Dems had started negotiations with Labour.

The main sticking point to a deal between the two parties ideologically closest to one another was removed early on:

Clegg: We won't even consider a coalition as long as Gordon Brown is still Labour leader.

Labour: Why have you handcuffed yourself to the radiator, Gordon?

Brown: I'm not going and that's that.

Labour: It's time to go.

Brown: I'm still the prime minister. I'm not resigning.

Labour: Of course you are, Gordon. And a very good job you are making of it, too. But we've got a really exciting new opportunity lined up for you . . .

Brown: I'm not going and that's that.

Labour: Get the bolt-cutters.

In the absence of a new government, Brown actually was still the prime minister at this point and much as he would have liked to have carried on – he'd waited long enough to get it, and to be kicked out of it on the very first occasion the voters were allowed their say on his competence must have been galling – he had to go. A coalition between Labour and the Lib Dems would have been discredited from the outset if Brown had been kept on. With the matter of the Labour leadership quickly resolved, the way ahead looked clear.

What happened over the next few days is open to various interpretations. Some called it the workings of a healthy democracy. Some saw it as the Lib Dems bargaining for the best outcome for the British people. Others saw it as the Lib

Dems angling for the best deal for themselves. The result was a coalition government between the Conservatives and the Lib Dems that only the most astute – or possibly cynical – observers would have predicted before the election.

The exact timings have also been a matter of debate. Some say that Labour dropped out of negotiations quite soon after securing Brown's exit, as there was a suspicion that the numbers still wouldn't add up even if they could form a coalition with the Lib Dems; even though the combined parties had enough seats to see off the Tories they still wouldn't have had an overall majority and would have had to rely on the support of the Scottish and Welsh nationalists to get their legislation through parliament. Under other, rosier circumstances that might not have been an insurmountable problem; but Labour knew that in May 2010 their own brand was fairly toxic to the public. The British people might not look too kindly on a deal that appeared as if it had been structured merely to extend the life of a Labour government that the voters had said they didn't want. If they lost an early vote in the Commons, there would be the prospect of a no-confidence vote in the government and another election within a year, at which Labour would almost certainly do even worse. Given that the Lib Dems were trying to play them off against the Tories for greater policy concessions and more Cabinet posts, and that the economy was in such a desperate state, the safest option might be to stay in opposition for five years. Let the Conservatives and the Lib Dems fail and let Labour come roaring back in 2015. That was the thinking, anyway . . .

With Labour out of the picture, there was only one other option and, as it became ever more likely, some Lib Dem supporters who had never seriously considered doing a deal with the Tories voiced their concerns. They went unheard, and confirmation of the deal between the Tories and the Lib Dems arrived late on the Tuesday – five days after the election – but not before Gordon Brown threw one last spanner in the works. He had known his time was up for a couple of days; the country had known his time was up for a couple of days. His humiliation was all too public, and his only remaining vestige of power was to force the Tories and the Lib Dems into a coalition before they had agreed all the fine details. With the furniture removers having almost finished packing up his possessions in Number 10, he cracked midway through the afternoon and phoned the Queen to say he would be coming along to Buckingham Palace shortly to resign formally as prime minister. 'Sod it,' he must have thought. 'I've had enough of being made to look an idiot while Cameron and Clegg prolong their flirting. If they can't make up their minds whether they're now an item or not, I can . . .'

With their minds duly concentrated, the Tories and the Lib Dems finalized their deal:

Cameron: The electorate has spoken and we have listened. So Nick and I have rolled up our sleeves and got on with the job of forming a coalition that will tackle the country's problems head on . . . etc.

Clegg: I agree with Dave. A time when the economy is facing its most serious crisis for nearly a century is no time to play party politics. It is vital for Britain's national interest that we should . . . etc.

Cameron talked a lot of 'rolling up his sleeves and getting on with the job' in his early Coalition speeches; sometimes he even did so. Rolling up your sleeves was the kind of thing upper-class men liked to do when there was work to be done: it made them feel as if they had experience of manual labour. Clegg's position was more ambiguous, though. He did have the further option of not forming a coalition with either party and letting the Conservatives rule as a minority government. The Lib Dems could have voted alongside the Tories on policy with which they agreed and either voted against or abstained on matters that were contrary to their stated manifesto. This would arguably have been the most ideologically pure position and might have put Cameron under more pressure than a coalition. Knowing that his minority government could be brought down at any moment, Cameron would have been forced to make sure every piece of legislation was sufficiently Lib Dem-friendly. What it wouldn't have done, of course, is given the Lib Dems any formal powers or responsibilities; they would have remained very much the third party.

Clegg cited the national interest as his reason for jumping into bed with an unexpected partner. Just what was the national interest, though? Was it something best served by the Lib Dems remaining on the outside and letting the Tories sink or swim? Or was it best served by the Lib Dems reaching a deal with the Tories that gave them both a chance in government? A deal that would invariably mean the Lib Dems sacrificing some of their principles? No matter what stability they gave the government or how much they tempered the Tories' policies, they were bound to be compromised at times. There was no getting round that. It's not unreasonable to imagine, therefore, that some of the coalition negotiations between Clegg and Cameron went more like this:

Cameron: Stop messing around. If we don't reach a deal then we're both toast . . .

Clegg: I can see you are. You'll go down in history as the man who had his chance and blew it. The Tories are an unforgiving bunch and if a minority government collapses in six months' time it will be 'Sayonara, Dave.' But I'll be OK either way.

Cameron: No, you won't. I've told the country I've made a big, comprehensive offer. This is it. Your one and only shot at real power for nearly a century. Say no and everyone will think you're a party of losers.

Clegg: What about my integrity?

Cameron: What about it? Do you really think your colleagues will remember that? They want a taste of power in the Cabinet every bit as much as you do. If you turn your back on this deal, then you're going to have to spend the rest of your political career – what little will remain – looking over your shoulder. Everyone will be briefing against you behind your back. 'Clegg bottled it, you know. He had a chance to take the Lib Dems forward but he lost his nerve. He preferred the easy option of shouting from the back benches . . .'

Clegg: But what about policy? We fundamentally disagree on so many issues . . .

Cameron: Who cares? This isn't about policy. It's about survival. As long as we talk a good game by saying we agree on the important issues . . .

Clegg: Like what?

Cameron: Oh, you know. The national interest: getting the country out of austerity, etc. That sort of thing. As long as we agree on this, the rest doesn't matter too much. If the worst comes to the worst we can always say we will both reach a compromise. That sounds mature. The punters will love it.

Clegg: You don't think everyone will eventually see through it?

Cameron: Probably. But by then it will be too late. This way we at least get five years at the top. If you say no, you get nothing and I will be lucky to get five months.

Clegg: Mmm. Put like that . . . But you do promise you won't shaft the Lib Dems when things get tricky?

Cameron: How could you imagine such a thing, Nick?

Clegg: And you are really, really interested in reforming the electoral system?

Cameron: Absolutely. Only this morning I was having a chat with William Hague about the benefits of proportional representation . . .

Disentangling who had got the better of the deal was not easy. Some thought Clegg had played a blinder and had secured far more power than he had a right to expect; others reckoned that the concessions Cameron had made would count for little once the business of governing began in earnest. All anyone could agree on was that was as harmonious as the Coalition would ever be. From this high point of *entente cordiale* between both parties, the only way was down. But first there was a marriage service to be held.

*

Exactly a week after the general election, two men – 'Call me Dave' and 'Call me Nick' – posed for the cameras outside Number 10 Downing Street. They looked for all the world like two men in love. So what if Nick's yellow tie clashed rather badly with his reddish hair? They smiled, they joked, they looked into each other's eyes, they touched each other reassuringly. Was this a political bromance? A new era of grown-up metrosexual politics?

Dave and Nick walked side by side through the building out into the Rose Garden at the back to give their first joint press conference as prime minister and deputy prime minister. Cameron spoke first about the new politics, careful to call it the Liberal Democrat–Conservative rather than the Conservative–Liberal Democrat Coalition, while Clegg looked on admiringly. Then it was Nick's turn: 'Liberalism is about giving young people the chance to be the people they want to be; giving them the opportunities they crave.' He could have been talking about himself at that minute.

There was one sticky moment when a reporter reminded Cameron that he had once described Clegg as his favourite political joke, but both leaders laughed it off as if they were a young royal couple giving a photo-call for the announce-ment of their engagement. 'Show us the ring, Nick!' 'Give him a kiss, Dave.' 'Aw shucks,' their demeanour suggested:

Cameron: It was just one of those silly things you say on the spur of the moment. It didn't mean anything . . .
Clegg: You know how it is when you're a bit embarrassed about admitting how much you fancy someone because you don't want people to laugh at you for being so keen? That's kind of how it was . . .

Nothing was going to spoil the day, not even the weather, which was unusually chilly for May. Two hearts spoke with one voice. Sometimes it was hard to tell them apart. 'Today we are not just announcing a new government and new ministers. We are announcing a new politics. A new politics where the national interest is more important than party interest. Where cooperation wins out over confrontation. Where compromise, give and take, reasonable, civilized, grown-up behaviour is not a sign of weakness but of strength,' said one. 'We have been through a campaign: now we have a coalition. That says a lot about the scale of the new politics which is now beginning to unfold. This is a new government and a new kind of government,' said the other. They could have been lovers finishing one another's sentences.

It was a love affair in which people wanted to believe. There was something refreshing, uplifting, about seeing two party leaders getting on with each other. Something hopeful after years of watching politicians at each other's throats, scoring cheap points and achieving . . . Well, what? The old tribal party politics hadn't been particularly effective in solving the economic crisis; maybe it was time to take a chance and try something new. Maybe the Coalition was the real deal.

But it was also a love affair that people couldn't help instinctively mistrusting. If both men were now so keen and enthusiastic about embracing a new form of politics, how come neither of them had bothered to mention it before? Clegg at least had talked of the possibility of a coalition – but not with Cameron, to whom he had always appeared ideologically opposed. And as for Cameron? That gag about

Clegg being his favourite political joke . . . Many a true word is said in jest.

There was also an undercurrent to the Rose Garden press conference that went beyond the natural delight of two men having pulled off a deal to create the first UK coalition government since the Second World War. A feeling that was slightly unnerving. For behind their smiles of excitement and satisfaction was a sense that neither of them could quite believe his luck. More than having just written their own get-out-of-jail-free cards for their political careers, Cameron and Clegg looked like kids who had both been given the keys to the best and most expensive train set in the world. What was worrying was that neither inspired much confidence that he knew how to make it work properly. Every new prime minister is, to some extent, a step into the unknown on the part of the electorate, but the Cameron–Clegg partnership felt like a massive leap of faith in a pair of men who looked more like boys:

Cameron: I can't believe it. All those people out there just for us . . .
Clegg: I know. I have to keep pinching myself as well.
Cameron: Go on, say it again . . .
Clegg: What?
Cameron: Call me Prime Minister.
Clegg: Good afternoon, Prime Minister.
Cameron: Good afternoon, Deputy Prime Minister.
Clegg: Who would have thought that we'd both end up here?
Cameron: Shall we go into the Cabinet Room?
Clegg: Isn't this great? Where will I be sitting? Next to you?
Cameron: Of course. What do you think this lever does?

Clegg: No idea. Why don't you pull it and see?
Cameron: Whoops. I've just drawn the curtains by mistake.

The novelty value of a coalition would buy both men a little time. But sooner rather than later they would have to deliver on the promises they had made. Not just to each other but to the country.

Chapter 5

Fight the Power

POLITICIANS RARELY DO THEMSELVES ANY FAVOURS, AND THAT'S especially true when they are trying to solicit our understanding. In recent years, many MPs have chosen to defend themselves against a growing disaffection with the political class by saying, 'I came into politics to make the world a better place.' This sounds good but is actually meaningless. How many people actively set out to make the world a worse place through their work? A few career criminals, genocidal dictators and hedge-fund managers. That's about it. Most of the rest of us would hope, at the very least, to leave the world no worse than we found it. Even if we fail miserably.

There are also a great many other careers that more obviously lend themselves to making the world a better place. Doctors, nurses, teachers, charity workers, for a start, most of whom don't rely on pointing out the failings of both their opponents and their colleagues as a means of achieving advancement. So expecting voters to buy into the notion of MPs as altruists, committed purely to public service, is a non-starter. Politicians may want to make the world a better place, but they are also a clear personality type. They are alpha men and women. People with large egos; possibly even borderline narcissists. People who need public recognition and attention, and can survive and enjoy a workplace that thrives on conflict. Unsurprisingly, many people suspect that it is a politician's personality at least as much as – if not rather more than – his or her finer feelings that determines career choice.

That said, most politicians are fairly decent people. They aren't the crooks and charlatans – well, not many of them – that they are often portrayed as being. They aren't any more stupid or more venal than the previous generation. There was no golden era when politicians were nobler and more morally upstanding; it's just that sexual infidelities and financial irregularities are much harder to keep quiet these days. The distinction between public and private life has been eroded, and voters expect politicians' private lives to be consistent with their public soundbites.

The fault-line that runs through almost every MP is the capacity for self-importance and self-delusion. A feeling that the normal rules don't apply inside the Palace of Westminster; that the consistency they would expect from themselves and their colleagues in other areas of life can be put on hold. Politics is known as the art of compromise: a world where you rarely get everything you want and end up settling for a lot less. A world where conscience and beliefs are frequently moving targets to be traded for some notion of a greater public good. A world in which, to rise to the front benches, MPs are often encouraged to promote a policy in which they don't wholeheartedly believe.

By and large, the public accepts this trade-off. We realize the world is imperfect and that policy is often influenced by pragmatism rather than ideals, and when we hear a politician defending the indefensible on the radio or TV we make allowances. We know we're being lied to, but don't necessarily assume the person telling the lie is fundamentally a liar. Though this does depend on the scale of the lie. It will be hard for many people on either the left or the right ever again to take anything Tony Blair says at face value now that his government's deception over the reasons for going to war with Iraq in 2003 has become clear.

What really gets to most people, though, is when MPs appear to be completely out of touch with the lives of those they are governing. When they are wittering on about what people want and what people should do without having any real experience of what it's like to be doing a job you don't particularly enjoy for an average national wage of £26,500. Not all MPs fall into this category; some have had jobs before becoming politicians, others have been trade-union activists. But there is now a growing cadre of younger career politicians who have next to no experience of anything but Westminster; who joined their chosen political party at school or university – almost always either Oxford or Cambridge – then became a special adviser, aka SPAD, to an MP on leaving university, before being fast-tracked and parachuted into a safe constituency. The problem for the Coalition was that both David Cameron and Nick Clegg fell squarely into the career-politician category.

It's said that David Cameron was ear-marked as a future prime minister by some of his teachers when he was at Eton. You could call this admirably far-sighted on behalf of the teachers who encouraged him in his ambition. Or you could call it just a bit surreal. Just how do you think those particular exchanges went?

Eton career adviser: So where do you see yourself in thirty years' time?

Cameron: I'm going to be prime minister when I grow up.

Eton career adviser: That sounds very reasonable. We'll give Tory Central Office a ring right now to let them know. Next, please.

Boris Johnson: Good evening, sir.

Eton career adviser: Ah! Johnson. What plans do you have for the future?

Johnson: I'm going to be prime minister.

Eton career adviser: Hmm. That could be a bit tricky because Cameron is going to do that. Would you settle for being a Cabinet minister or a captain of industry . . . ?

Johnson: No.

Eton career adviser: London mayor?

Johnson: *No.*

Eton career adviser: Well, OK then. If you insist. But you will have to wait until Cameron has had his turn.

Wouldn't the more normal conversation at a less privileged school have gone more like this?

Cameron: I'm going to be prime minister when I grow up.

Teachers: And that's a very good thing to aspire to, David. Now what else do you think you might like to do?

Cameron: I'm serious. I'm going to be prime minister.

Teachers: Of course you are. But let's just say that something terrible happens. You do realize that only one person in the country can be prime minister at any one time?

Cameron: Of course I do. I'm not stupid.

Teachers: We weren't saying you are stupid, David. We're just saying that it could be a good idea to have back-up plans in case becoming prime minister doesn't work out. Have you thought about estate management? Your future wife may have a fair bit of land that needs looking after. Or how about insurance?

The issue is one of entitlement and expectation. The Eton careers advice was perfectly sensible because becoming prime minister was entirely plausible. Cameron was bright, a Tory, socially accomplished, ambitious and well-connected. Why shouldn't he become prime minister? Someone has to be prime minister, so why not him?

After leaving Eton, Cameron followed the seamless, predestined trajectory to Downing Street. He went to Oxford, where he got a first in politics, philosophy and economics (PPE), the degree *de nos jours* for any aspiring politico, and, on graduating, went to work in the Conservative Research Department. From there he was seconded to Downing Street, before going to work as a special adviser to both the chancellor of the exchequer and the home secretary. Having made it on to the approved list of Conservative parliamentary candidates, Cameron resigned as a special adviser to become director of corporate affairs for Carlton TV while he waited for the right seat to turn up. He was first selected for the marginal constituency of Stafford, but lost the 1997 election, before graduating at the 2001 election to Witney, traditionally a safe Conservative seat but at the time held by Labour after its MP, Sean Woodward, had defected from the Tories in 1999. Cameron returned it to the fold and within two years he was a shadow minister; within three he was on the shadow front bench; and within four he was leader of his party.

Nick Clegg's rise to the top had a similar appearance of inevitability. He attended Westminster, a top private school, then went on to Cambridge University, where he studied social anthropology and joined the Conservative party. Clegg has always said he has no knowledge of this, though the records suggest otherwise. Perhaps it was just a trial run for the Coalition. At some point during his time at Cambridge, he must have realized that not doing PPE had put his political career at a disadvantage and signed up to do a Masters degree in the US to compensate. After a year's internship on the *Nation*, a liberal political magazine in New York, he did a further Masters degree in Bruges – just in case the first one wasn't good enough – spent two years working for a political lobbying group, and then took a post with the European Commission in Brussels. He became a Lib Dem MEP in 1999 and five years later was selected to represent his party in the Sheffield Hallam constituency when the incumbent MP, Richard Allan, announced his intention to stand down at the next election. Clegg was elected in 2005, became the Lib Dems' home affairs spokesman the following year and its leader the year after that.

If the route to the top had actually been quite tough for both men, that's not the way it looked from the outside. Neither appeared to have had to struggle for anything very much. Neither had had much of a life outside a privileged, metropolitan existence: the jobs they had done looked very much as if they were stepping stones on the way to the top that had been thoughtfully placed in their path, rather than positions that were valued or desired in themselves.

While Cameron and Clegg were quietly pinching themselves in Number 10 before their Rose Garden appearance –

'Can you believe we're actually in charge?' – the nation did its own double-take soon afterwards. The country was going through its worst economic crisis for nearly a hundred years, and the two men on whom we were relying to pull us through were comparative ingénus with little experience of anything except being politicians. Neither had noticeably suffered under the financial collapse, but both felt qualified to tell the nation, 'We're all in this together.' Rarely had the disconnect between the governed and the governors felt so acute.

The price the Conservatives had had to pay for the Coalition was soon clear. Five of the twenty-one remaining key Cabinet positions – Cameron and Clegg had already formalized their roles as prime minister and deputy prime minister – went to the Lib Dems. They weren't any of the top jobs, such as chancellor, foreign secretary or home secretary, but they were still five influential posts that the Tories might have expected to fill before the election. Which left five senior Tories feeling as if they had been passed over. Cameron and Clegg might have been all smiles in the Rose Garden as they celebrated the birth of a new form of politics, but the sweetness and light was just a little bit sourer elsewhere. Many Conservatives thought the Lib Dems had been handed at least one too many Cabinet posts – but even they couldn't have imagined the Lib Dems would be a man down inside three weeks.

David Laws had been one of the principal architects of the Coalition. As one of the more right-wing Lib Dem MPs, he had been one of those closest to having a foot in both camps: a man who could be trusted by both sides. His reward for having brokered the deal was a place in the Cabinet as chief secretary to the Treasury, with a remit to cut public spending. It might have been a good idea if he had started by curbing his personal spending from the public purse.

The parliamentary expenses scandal had first been exposed by the *Daily Telegraph* almost exactly a year before. Day after day in May 2009, the newspaper revealed some of the more outrageous expenses claims that MPs had submitted over the previous ten years or so – most of which had been approved. By a committee of MPs, of course. Who else? Some of these claims were almost comical: Sir Peter Viggers had claimed £1,645 for a duck island; Michael Gove £134.50 for elephant lamps; and John Reid £1.50 for an ice-cube tray. David Cameron had claimed back the cost of having the wisteria removed from his country home, while Douglas Hogg had got the taxpayer to pay for having his moat cleaned. Many claims, though, were borderline – sometimes actually – criminal, with MPs working the system by 'flipping' their houses – changing the designation of their second homes in order to maximize tax allowances:

MP's spouse: Where are we living this week, darling?
MP: Not really sure?
MP's spouse: Well, if it's all the same to you, I'd rather say we were living in our other house. There are some lovely new curtains I'm buying and parliament is offering us an incredibly good deal on expenses.

Incredibly, this was something that the Members' Expenses Committee had actively encouraged.

Predictably, many MPs' first reaction was to go on the

defensive. 'This is just s-s-o-o-o unfair. You don't understand how hard it is for us,' was a common refrain – one caused by the fact that most MPs felt they were terribly underpaid. Unlike almost everyone else in the country, MPs had, up to this point, always been in the fortunate position of voting on their own pay and, while not exactly allowing themselves to go short, even they had come to realize it would be a PR disaster if they were consistently to award themselves salary increases that outstripped everyone else in the country. So they had repeatedly taken the high-minded decision to award themselves only modest pay rises – their pension increases were rather less high-minded, but that's another story – and by 2010 the basic salary for an ordinary backbencher was about £65,000. Rather more than most people earned, but considerably less than they felt they were worth.

The expenses kicked in as a semi-official top-up system. In lieu of salary, there were generous levels of bonuses on offer, taking in everything from furnishing allowances, accommodation, travel and almost anything else an imaginative mind could dream up. And as parliament didn't require members to provide receipts for any trifling items under the value of £250, MPs from both sides of the House became extremely financially creative. It's not something you could imagine happening in any other workplace:

Manager: Excuse me . . .
Shop assistant: What do you want?
Manager: I was just wondering what you were doing with those lamp shades?
Shop assistant: I was taking them home.
Manager: Have you paid for them?

Shop assistant: Don't be silly. They're a perk of the job. You're having a laugh if you think I'm going to work for you on the minimum wage without a few extras, know what I mean?

Manager: Er . . .

Shop assistant: Look, they're well under £250 the pair, so no harm done. And while you're about it, would you mind shelling out for the mortgage payments on my second home? Between you and me, it's more my first home really, but since the outgoings are a lot higher on this one, it makes sense to call it my second one, if you get my meaning.

Manager: Ah! Now you put it like that, I understand perfectly. Would you like someone to carry those lamp shades out to your car?

Shop assistant: That's most helpful, my good man.

Manager: You've forgotten the receipt . . .

But that's the way it was in the House of Commons up until 2009. Providing MPs played along with the very generous rules, it was also entirely legal. Even when anomalies were pointed out, there was little come-back. In 2007, Ed Balls and Yvette Cooper – a married couple who were also Labour Cabinet ministers – were accused of manipulating the system to buy a £665,000 house: the complaint was dismissed as the couple had acted within the rules. A year later, two married Conservative MPs, Nicholas and Ann Winterton, were accused of claiming back mortgage interest on a mortgage they had already repaid. This time the Committee on Standards and Privileges did find there had been a breach of the rules, but they weren't asked to repay the money. Nice work if you can get it. So it went on. Caroline Spelman was found to have 'inadvertently' claimed for a nanny. Jacqui Smith identified her main home as one in which she often spent only two days a week. Eric Pickles claimed for a second home that was just 37 miles – a distance considerably less than many people commute daily – from his main home. But he is quite large, so perhaps he had reasons connected with his health. Parliament was happy to give him the benefit of the doubt at any rate.

When the *Daily Telegraph* exposed the expenses scandal, most MPs put their hands up in surrender. Not to say embarrassment. Most were quick to dip into their pockets and repay some of their expenses – David Cameron paid back £1,000 – while saying, 'We can see this looks very bad. It is time to put our house in order.' None, though, volunteered an explanation for why they had thought the expenses system was perfectly acceptable before each MP's individual claims were put on general show.

As a sign that they were willing to respond to the criticism, MPs set up the Independent Parliamentary Standards Authority (IPSA) later in 2009 to monitor their expenses; shortly before the 2010 general election, IPSA was also handed responsibility for deciding MPs' pay. So, given the high levels of mistrust with which politicians were viewed and the fact that David Cameron was trying to portray the Coalition as a new era of open politics, it might have been expected that he would have had a chat with his prospective Cabinet ministers before their appointment:

Cameron: OK, everyone. I'm sorry to have to get you all in here like this, but I've got to ask if there's anything in your past that might be considered – how can I put it? – a little bit iffy that might come back to bite us?

Everyone: There is that photo of you, George Osborne and Boris Johnson looking like a right bunch of posh numpties in the Bullingdon Club.
Cameron: Yes, yes. Never mind that . . .
Everyone: And there is the photo of George sitting next to an S&M dominatrix with what looks to be a small pile of cocaine in front of her . . .
Cameron: Minor details . . . I was thinking rather more of any financial irregularities. Anyone got any tax deals I should know about?
Osborne: Well . . . the family trust fund is kept offshore.
Cameron: That's just shrewd tax planning. People will admire that in a chancellor. Now, how about ongoing expenses . . . er . . . difficulties? However trivial. Best to get it out now . . . Anyone?
(*Silence*)
Cameron: Speak now or for ever hold your peace . . .
(*Silence*)
Cameron: David . . . have you got anything you'd like to add here?
Laws: Mmm. Nothing that comes immediately to mind.
Cameron: Are you certain about that?
Laws: Absolutely. A hundred and ten per cent.
Cameron: That's all splendid then. Consider yourselves all in the Cabinet.

In less than three weeks, David Laws was out of the Cabinet after the *Daily Telegraph* revealed he had claimed more than £40,000 in second-home expenses over a five-year period between 2004 and 2009, during which time he had been renting a room from his partner, James Lundie. This was banned under parliamentary rules that had been established in 2006. Laws maintained he had broken the rules only in order to keep his sexuality private and had not sought any financial gain, but he resigned as chief secretary to the Treasury anyway. Though his resignation may have been more of a case of jumping to avoid being pushed.

A year later, when the Standards and Privileges Committee investigation into Laws's expenses claims had been completed, he was found to have made six serious breaches of parliamentary rules. Not only were his rental claims misleading, they had been in excess of market rents. His claims for phone bills and building works were also found to be irregular. As punishment, Laws was suspended from the House of Commons for seven days; he returned to government as a junior education minister the following year, 2012.

For Cameron to have made such an avoidable mistake in appointing Laws to the Cabinet without getting his staff to do a thorough background check was a serious lapse of judgement, one that betrayed his inexperience. At a time when he badly needed to restore confidence in the integrity of government, he had given more ammunition to those who thought that, however idealistic and high-minded MPs might sound in public, in private they found the opportunities of lining their own pockets irresistible.

Four years later, Cameron's judgement was still in question. The expenses scandal had continued to unravel throughout the life of the Coalition government, with some former MPs – all from the Labour benches, though most people outside the judicial system couldn't detect any difference between what they had done and what Conservative MPs had done – being sent to prison on charges of fraud and false accounting. The last investigation to be completed was that of the Conservative culture secretary, Maria Miller, its delay in resolution being almost entirely due to her efforts to obstruct it. Indeed, Miller's special adviser, Joanna Hindley, had phoned the *Daily Telegraph* – which had once again broken the story – to try to warn them off by reminding the newspaper that Miller was in charge of enacting any legislation in regard to the Leveson Inquiry into press regulation. Of which more – much more – later.

In February 2014, the independent standards commissioner, Kathryn Hudson, found that Maria Miller had over-claimed on her second-home allowance and ruled she should repay £45,000. MPs on the Standards Committee thought about this for the best part of a month before concluding that Hudson had been a wee bit harsh; they decided instead that Miller need repay only £5,800 and apologize to the House of Commons. Maria Miller's statement lasted just thirty-two seconds. It wasn't quite as short as Tory MP Nadine Dorries's apology for trousering her fee for her appearance on the TV show *I'm A Celebrity, Get Me Out of Here!*, but its subtext was the same:

Speaker: Order, order! The secretary of state for culture wishes to make a personal statement.
Miller: Yeah, whatever.

Had Miller made a fuller apology, one that sounded as if she understood she was at fault and that the public were angry about it, she might have survived.

Just as curious as her non-apology was David Cameron's decision publicly to back his minister. The affair dragged on for another week – re-opening many of the old sores about the venality of politicians that everyone in parliament might have hoped had been largely forgotten, if not healed – before Miller was forced to resign. It was almost as if there was something self-destructively Pavlovian in the government's response. At the very least it proved there was still a huge gulf between the House of Commons's idea of being in touch with the ordinary people and the ordinary people's perception of what being in touch actually meant.

That wasn't quite the end of the expenses embarrassment for Cameron. In August 2014 Mark Simmonds, a junior minister in the foreign office, resigned from government because the new punitive level of parliamentary expenses made it impossible for him to bring up his family in London. Simmonds earned £89,000 as a government minister, claimed £28,000 in rental allowance and paid his wife up to £25,000 from his staff allowance to be his office manager. And still he couldn't quite get by. The maximum housing benefit the Coalition government allowed a claimant for a three-bedroomed flat in inner London was £18,249. His resignation did nothing to allay fears that many politicians had no idea how ordinary people lived.

Chapter 6

Money, Money, Money

GEORGE OSBORNE FACED AN EVEN BIGGER BATTLE THAN DAVID Cameron to portray himself as both a man of the people and the man to save Britain. Like Cameron, he had had a privileged Home Counties background – son of a baronet, St Paul's, Oxford, the Bullingdon Club – from which he had eased himself effortlessly into the Tory party, first as a member of the Central Office back-room team and then as an up-and-coming MP. David Cameron had appointed him shadow chancellor of the exchequer at the age of thirty-three and now, five years later as chancellor, he was the man tasked with steering Britain through the worst recession for nearly a hundred years. His only apparent qualifications and experience for the job were a history degree and insider knowledge of the workings of the Conservative party.

Unlike Cameron, Osborne had little personal charm. Where Cameron had the easy patrician confidence of some-one who believed the lower orders were intrinsically 'good eggs' and was happy to prove it by going into a pub and buy-ing a pint, Osborne looked like someone who would rather avoid all contact with anyone from outside his immediate social circle at all costs. His lips curled into a natural sneer, his voice was shrill and his eyes held little warmth; it could have been shyness, but the public weren't prepared to give him the benefit of the doubt after it was revealed that he had had dinner on the private yacht of Russian oligarch Oleg Deripaska while on holiday in Corfu in 2008 with his close friend, the banker Nathaniel Rothschild.

Almost as bad as being caught schmoozing with a banker and an oligarch was the presence at this dinner of Labour Cabinet minister Peter Mandelson. Mandelson was something of a curiosity: a politician remarkable as much for having been forced to resign from the Cabinet on two occasions as for being appointed to it three times; a man greatly admired by many within Westminster for his nous and connections, but who was almost universally mistrusted by the outside world. Just being seen in Mandelson's company brought its own assumptions of guilt. Of what, no one knew or much cared, but if Mandelson was involved then there had to be a hidden purpose. Rothschild suggested Osborne had been trying to solicit funds from Deripaska for the Conservative party's election campaign. Osborne denied this. They can't both have been right.

Come the election in 2010, Osborne's personal ratings were still dismal. People just didn't like him. So much so that the Tories did their best to keep Osborne away from the voters for the duration of the campaign:

Conservatives: Labour has totally mismanaged the economy.
Media: Can George Osborne spell out your party's plans for cutting the deficit?
Conservatives: Er, we've got Chris Grayling here, if that helps. I'm sure he can run through a few things for you.

Media: It's not really the shadow home secretary we're after . . .

Conservatives: Mmm, I see where you're coming from. How about David Cameron, then? We could get him to have a word with you in a couple of hours or so.

Media: No. This is very much Osborne's field. We want to speak to him.

Conservatives: Well, you can't.

Media: Why not?

Conservatives: Because you can't.

Media: Why not?

Conservatives: Er . . . because he's just gone out.

Media: No, he hasn't. We know he's in there . . .

Osborne: No, I'm not.

Media: We knew he was in.

Osborne: I'm not. I'm a pre-recorded voice.

Media: Come on, George. Out you come!

Conservatives: Oh look, David's free now. Would you like to talk to David?

The policy worked. Osborne's media outings were heavily restricted and whatever damage Central Office feared he might inflict was contained. But now that the election had been won and Osborne was chancellor of the exchequer, inevitably he became more visible. Within days of assuming office, he established an independent Office for Budget Responsibility (OBR) to analyse the nation's finances. Either the UK had very little money left to count – Liam Byrne, Labour's outgoing chief secretary to the Treasury had left a cheeky note for his successor that read, 'Dear Chief Secretary, I'm afraid there is no money. Kind regards – and good luck!'

– or the OBR worked at breakneck speed, for within seven weeks Osborne delivered his emergency budget.

'This is the unavoidable budget,' Osborne told parliament. That statement was slightly disingenuous, depending on your understanding of the word 'unavoidable'. It was more or less the sort of budget that Osborne had been hinting he would deliver while he was in opposition, but it didn't look much like the budget that his Lib Dem Coalition colleagues had had in mind during their election campaign. If Nick Clegg had been the poster boy for the Lib Dems, Vince Cable had been the party's principled, intellectual heavyweight. Cable had talked convincingly about the state of the country's finances and the need to curb the power of the bankers, and there were many who thought he would make a far sounder chancellor than either Osborne or Labour's shadow chancellor, Ed Balls. He gave the impression of being someone who would make the right decisions, however difficult, rather than ones that suited a narrow party-political ideology.

Which is to say, Cable was a potential problem for Osborne. The last thing the new chancellor needed was for a more experienced, more popular politician to be stomping all over his patch. Equally, the Coalition couldn't be seen to be obviously excluding Cable from his areas of expertise: that wouldn't send out the message that the Coalition was a new world of non-partisan pooling of talent. So Cable had been made secretary of state for business, innovation and skills – a Cabinet position that was connected with the economy but also kept him at arm's length from day-to-day decision-making. There weren't many signs that Cable had been included in Osborne's pre-budget talks:

Cable: We need to talk about the budget.
Osborne: We do?
Cable: Yes. I'm very keen to be involved.
Osborne: OK . . . When are you free?
Cable: I've got Tuesday and Wednesday next week clear.
Osborne: Mmm. Let me see . . . No, that's not going to work. I've got a school sports day on Tuesday, and on Wednesday I'm going to the dentist. How about the weekend?
Cable: 'Fraid not. I have to be in Brussels.
Osborne: Shame . . . I could have given you fifteen minutes on Saturday morning. But don't worry. You'll love the budget, I promise you.

Would he? The Lib Dems might have been slightly consoled that their proposals on changes to capital gains tax had been included in a very watered-down form, but there was little else for them to cheer, as the budget that Osborne delivered was pretty much a straightforward austerity Conservative budget. Public spending was to be cut by £6 billion, and a million public sector jobs were to be axed; the progressive measure of raising the income threshold at which people would start paying income tax was more than nullified by a 2.5 per cent hike in VAT – an increase that would hit the low-paid much harder than those on bigger salaries.

The Lib Dems had little choice but to support the budget in public and hope for the best. They would, at least, be in a state of grace for a short time between its delivery and its repercussions. There's one rule in government that overrides all others: get all the unpleasant, tricky decisions over and done with early on while you've still got the public's goodwill and while you can blame the incompetence of the previous government for the necessity of your actions. Hopefully, so the theory goes, the voters will have forgotten most of the pain you've inflicted on them by the time the next election comes around – especially if you toss them a few feel-good bones in the last year or so of the parliament. The only dangers are delay and carrying on blaming your predecessors for too long: if you're still blaming the previous government for failings in the economy four years into your own term of office, then there's a fair chance you've failed to address the problem yourself.

Not that this stops politicians from doing so: blame is a reflex response at Westminster. When Labour was attacking the government for selling off the Royal Mail too cheaply in 2014, the Coalition brought up Gordon Brown's decision to sell off the Treasury's gold reserves at rock-bottom prices between 1999 and 2002. Even as a deflectionary tactic this had little going for it, and as a coherent argument it was a non-starter. There was no connection between selling off the gold reserves and the Royal Mail: one being an error didn't excuse the other. If being 100 per cent right was a pre-condition for offering criticism, then parliament would be almost silent.

As a basic action plan for the first year of government, though, blaming the previous incumbents for your actions is near faultless, because its premise is entirely credible. After all, if the previous government had been doing a decent job and the economy had been ticking over quite nicely, then it would have been re-elected to carry on as per usual. Labour had failed to get the country out of the economic mess, there-fore it was only fair to let the Conservatives have a go at doing it their way. Call it the British sense of fair play in action.

Except the more telling – and seldom asked – question was not whether Labour had messed up or whether the Coalition would do any better, but whether any government could have done any better at the time. Broadly speaking, a chancellor used to have two means of controlling the economy: fiscal and monetarist policy. Both of these instruments were relatively blunt. Fiscal policy raised money for the government to spend on the NHS, schools, social services and infrastructure projects, and aimed to stimulate the health of the economy by ensuring the preconditions were in place for everyone to do well and create wealth. Monetarist policy aimed to keep inflation in check by putting the emphasis on control of the money supply through the reduction or increase of interest rates. Since Gordon Brown had handed over control of interest rates to the Bank of England in 1997, chancellors had been limited to just fiscal policy. The key driver here was how much revenue could a government bring in through tax receipts and what it would then do with the money. Spend it on public services? Or cut spending to pay off government debt?

Traditionally, fiscal policies – especially increasing taxation – had always been the starting point of Labour's economic policy, while Margaret Thatcher's Conservative government of 1979–90 had made monetarism its core strategy. Since the mid-1990s, though, there had been – if not in rhetoric, as the Labour party still had to look as if it was on the side of working people and the Tories still needed to appeal to their core Middle England free-market supporters – some economic rapprochement between the two main parties.

The Conservatives had discovered that having a softer, more caring side – apart from limiting the chances of the civil disorder that had punctuated the 1980s – was a vote-winner with the electorate, while Labour, under the leadership of Tony Blair, had found it rather liked the idea of personal wealth. In the Harold Wilson government of the 1960s the highest rate of tax had been the pre-decimal-currency equivalent of 90p in the pound; under Blair and Brown it had remained at 40p in the pound, apart from a brief rise to 50p for anyone earning over £150,000 in April 2010, in response to a feeling among the public that the bankers who had caused many of the economic problems were still getting away with it and needed to be punished.

The 50p rate of tax was largely symbolic, as the extra revenues it brought in were marginal. There weren't huge numbers of people earning more than £150,000, and the extra 10p in the pound collected didn't add up to a great deal once taxpayers had taken steps to avoid paying the extra costs. More tellingly, the extremely rich didn't have to pay at all. If you were one of the suckers paying tax at 50p on your earnings over £150,000, then you really weren't that rich after all. When Peter Mandelson said in 1998 that the New Labour government was 'intensely relaxed about people getting filthy rich', he meant it. He qualified the remark by adding 'as long as they pay their taxes': this he didn't mean quite so much.

Over the last twenty years or so, the extremely rich had become a small, virtually tax-exempt, clique of their own. Businesspeople were able to get away with paying almost no income tax by channelling their company's earnings into offshore tax jurisdictions. Exact figures are hard to come by, but it is reckoned most billionaires pay a personal rate of tax of about 10p in the pound. Suddenly having your own island in the Caribbean starts to look almost affordable.

The reason the super-rich get away with paying so little tax is not just because they are the ones who can afford the best accountants to dream up avoidance schemes; it's because government politicians let them get away with it. Men like Tony Blair and David Cameron find the company of the very rich extremely seductive. Power attracts power and the self-delusions set in. We can't ask the very rich to pay any more. They've already done so much for the country by creating businesses that employ so many people. Wouldn't it be awful if these philanthropic tycoons were to get the hump because we asked them to pay more tax and relocated their businesses elsewhere? The super-rich simply smile their cheesy, sun-kissed smiles and say nothing. They don't need to say anything. The threat is enough.

Nor is it just individuals who are tax-exempt. Big multinationals, such as Amazon, Google and Vodafone, pay a tiny proportion of their profits in corporation tax to the UK government because they can channel their money through offshore subsidiaries. When an ordinary individual has dealings with Her Majesty's Revenue and Customs officials, the conversation tends to go like this:

HMRC: We've detected an anomaly in your tax return.
Individual: Really?
HMRC: Yes. You've failed to declare all the income you received from the whip-round when you were made redundant. By our estimates, your liability has been increased by £17.85. Please pay as soon as possible as interest is accruing on this outstanding amount.

With large corporations the tone of the conversation is more relaxed:

HMRC: So how much did you make last year?
Vodafone: It's very hard to say . . .
HMRC: Just roughly . . .
Vodafone: Well, we had a turnover of about £5 billion, but we only seem to have made a profit of £11.32.
HMRC: That's very bad luck . . .
Vodafone: Isn't it just?
HMRC: How much tax would you like to pay, then?
Vodafone: Nothing.
HMRC: If you insist . . .
Vodafone: But as we love this country – we really do – we'll give you £20 million providing you stop bothering us . . .
HMRC: I say! That's most terribly generous.

That last sweetheart deal was conducted on George Osborne's watch, but Labour had been equally understanding on tax matters with other companies. On many economic issues, the differences between the two parties were primarily ones of rhetoric rather than substance. After the financial crash, Osborne had been quick to blame Labour for failing to regulate the financial-services industry sufficiently – which might have been a fair criticism had not the Conservatives been equally in favour of financial deregulation at the time.

It wasn't a coincidence that the more extreme fiscal policies of Old Labour and the hard-line monetarism of the Thatcher government had both shifted to more of a middle ground. The middle ground was where the floating voters tended to be located and it made no political sense to polarize opinion by pursuing policies that mainly appealed to a hard-core support that was always going to vote for you anyway. Likewise, the power of the trade unions had been in steady decline since the Thatcher years: most of the old manufacturing industries had died and the notion of what constituted the traditional working class had become a moving target. Politicians now won more votes by talking about consensus, hard-working people and aspiration than they did by stirring up class warfare.

But that wasn't all. For a long time, a government's policy had a direct – if not always intended – impact on the country's economic activity. Since the growth of a more global economy, however, the success or failure of a country's economy had as much – if not more – to do with what was going on elsewhere in the world as with any direction imposed on it by its own government. There were exceptions. Norway had a small population and huge reserves of oil, making it almost immune to both global recession and any screw-ups its politicians might make. With its huge wealth of natural resources, Australia fell into the same category. But the UK most definitely didn't. Most of the income generated by North Sea oil had been long since spent and the reserves were limited. And while not having joined the euro had offered the UK some protection against the meltdown in the Eurozone countries, it wasn't enough to stave off the effects of a global recession.

This was something politicians understood but couldn't properly admit, as telling the truth was not a real option:

Osborne: This emergency budget of mine . . .
The country: Yes?

Osborne: Well, I'm not entirely sure it's going to work as well as I said it would . . .

The country: What? You sounded very confident at the time.

Osborne: I know, I know. But I had to. If I'd said, 'Look, guys, I've given it my best shot, but the UK just isn't that big a global power any more. All the big money is in the US, China and the Eurozone. And Russia and India. So a lot really depends on how well they get their acts together. If America and the Eurozone stay fucked, then we pretty much stay fucked too.

The country: So what you're saying is that all these austerity measures may not make much difference?

Osborne: They may, they may not. I just don't know . . . I hope so. I mean, they seemed like a good idea at the time . . . Look, I can try and help businesses grow but, in the end, if they all go tits up because of global problems, what can I do?

The country: And?

Osborne: It would be nice if we could increase exports, but that's not wholly in my hands either . . .

The country: And those new private-sector jobs you promised would appear for all those who lost their public-sector jobs?

Osborne: Same thing, really. Look, if it all works out OK, I will take the credit. And if it doesn't, then I'll blame the rest of the world. And Labour, of course . . .

The country: And how about if it turns out that your policies were wrong but the country recovered anyway thanks to the rest of the world recovering?

Osborne: That's a category error. That's just not going to happen.

There are two commonly accepted strategies for getting an economy out of recession. The first is for the government to carry on public spending in the hope that it will stimulate recovery through growth; the second is to cut spending to reduce the deficit – the difference between tax revenues and spending commitments – in order to begin balancing the books. Labour had begun the deficit reduction the previous year – in early 2010 Britain had the highest budget deficit of all EU countries, even Greece – but Osborne's budget ratcheted up the scale of the cuts further than Labour had been prepared to go. And further than the Lib Dems would have wanted, because the dangers of excessive austerity measures were that they could stall any recovery indefinitely and that the economy would merely continue to bump along in a recession.

All in all, the budget was not one the Lib Dems would ordinarily have sanctioned, but the extremity of the economic recession and the newness of the Coalition gave them some political leeway. There was a general willingness in the country to accept that austerity had become an inevitability; a bit like going to war with Germany in 1939, it was something that had to be done. The real dilemma for the Lib Dems was getting people to feel that the cuts and the pain would be distributed evenly across all parts of society. If they could manage that, then most things would be forgiven.

It was a hard act to pull off. The new mantra of the Coalition became 'We're all in this together', and to make the point David Cameron would frequently take his jacket off before making a speech in public. It was his nod to the common man, because taking off your jacket was what ordinary people did – just as they (like the prime minister) often rolled up their sleeves. Both these phrases remain in Cameron's repertoire to this day.

They quickly became empty tics rather than slogans, though. Few people ever really felt we were all in this together. They looked at the Coalition Cabinet – and the political class in general – and saw a group of people who seemed quite comfortably off and largely immune to their own austerity measures. Osborne himself had a 15 per cent stake in his family's interior-design and wallpaper company and an estimated private net worth in excess of £4.5 million. It wasn't a great look for a chancellor during an economic recession. Osborne was by no means the only offender. A report by Wealth-X, a consultancy specializing primarily in the financial affairs of US politicians, found that eighteen of the twenty-nine members of the Coalition who attended Cabinet meetings were millionaires and that their collective wealth was about £70 million.

The real pain of the government's austerity measures was being felt a great deal further down the food chain. The main sufferers were those right at the bottom, those on benefits or working part-time in minimum-wage jobs. The Tory side of the Coalition didn't feel too bad about this, as there had long been a feeling on the right wing of the party that most people on benefits were idle scroungers who were taking the piss out of a system that rewarded them for not working. For them, the cuts in benefit spending were every bit as much a moral as a financial imperative:

Tories: Come on out, you scroungers. We know you're hiding indoors watching your 40-inch high-definition TVs and drinking lager all day. You're probably taking drugs, too.

We think it's about time you got off your backsides and got a proper job. So we're going to smoke you out by reducing your benefits until you are forced to get a job.

This message actually went down quite well in many areas, as it chimed with a view of the welfare system held by a large number of people. However, those who thought the benefits system was a help-yourself free-for-all were not, by and large, the claimants themselves. While there were a few well-publicized cases of people abusing the system, most of those on benefits were struggling to get by – they were people who either couldn't work because of health issues or wanted to work but were unable to find a job.

The key flaw in the Coalition's logic was the premise that there were all these jobs out there waiting to be filled by people who were now claiming benefits. Part of Osborne's 2010 election promise was that one million new, well-paid jobs would be created in the private sector. These jobs stubbornly refused to appear in either 2011 or 2012, and the ones that did were mainly offering a minimum wage or zero-hours contracts that provided no fixed income or long-term security. In the recovery from austerity, the Coalition had actually made the poorest members of society just that bit poorer. An interesting definition of 'We're all in this together.'

George Osborne had always insisted there was 'No Plan B' for the economy. The recovery would be his way or no way. For some years it seemed it was destined to be no way. Almost month upon month, the chancellor was forced to revise his forecasts downwards as the economic data refused to match his expectations. By 2011 growth was down by

2 per cent and inflation up by 5 per cent. The austerity period that Osborne had said would officially end by 2014–15 – conveniently in time for the election – had been put back by three years.

For the Coalition this was more of an inconvenience and an embarrassment than a disaster, as it still fell within the customary period of grace allowed for blaming the previous government. But the inconvenience and embarrassment were growing. There was rioting in the streets in August 2011 – not the full-scale riots of the Thatcher era, more opportunistic looting, but still an unwelcome reminder of a latent discontent. More disturbing was the fact that many people on average incomes were getting poorer and poorer. Wage rises didn't match the increase in the cost of living, so more and more families were finding their personal budgets had become stretched.

The Coalition's answer to this was semantics. Cabinet ministers began to differentiate between 'working people' and 'hard-working people'. It was no longer good enough just to be a working person. A working person was someone who was inherently a bit lazy; someone who was working only because the government had forced them into it and was looking for every opportunity to skive off from their zero-hours-contract job. A hard-working person was someone rather more middle class; someone with a white-collar job, a mortgage – kids, preferably – who now found that their income didn't stretch quite as far as it used to and was understandably a bit pissed off about it.

In essence, the difference between working people and hard-working people was a moral one. The difference between the undeserving poor and the deserving poor. It was also one that rapidly became an implicit part of the political debate as even Labour politicians started using the phrase 'hard-working people' as part of their own everyday rhetoric. It was almost as if they were worried that, were they not to do so, the middle classes – or 'squeezed middle' as they had also become known – might think Labour didn't feel their pain.

The 2012 budget marked a nadir for the Coalition. Not only was there still no sign of the promised economic recovery, but their presentational skills lapsed into farce. It started with George Osborne raising VAT on hot takeaway foods, a measure that quickly became known as the 'Pasty Tax' because it appeared to be aimed primarily at the working classes. Labour had a field day:

Labour: When did you last eat a pasty?
Osborne: What's a pasty?
Labour: That pie you've just taxed.
Osborne: I don't think I've ever knowingly eaten something like that. But from what you've told me it doesn't sound terribly nice and people who eat this sort of thing probably deserve to pay a little more for being so reckless.
Cameron: I love pasties, me . . .
Labour: Sorry?
Cameron: I'm a man of the people. I love pasties. I eat them all the time. In fact I can't stop eating them . . .
Labour: So when did you last have a pasty?
Cameron: Oh. Let me think. Yes, that's it. I had a fantastic one on Leeds station recently . . .
Labour: There isn't a pasty shop on Leeds station.
Cameron: That's odd. I could have sworn it was Leeds.

Maybe it was Liverpool.
Labour: There isn't one there either.
Cameron: Luton?
Labour: No.
Cameron: I've got it! It was Looe. I knew it began with L. Sam and I shared one on the beach while we were on hols in Cornwall a couple of years ago.

Cameron's efforts to salvage the situation with his common touch only made things worse. There was more budget trouble around the corner when the petrol-tanker drivers threatened to go on strike in protest against the government's proposed rise in fuel duty. It had been a tanker-drivers' strike that had given Blair's government several of its worst weeks in 2000. Long queues on garage forecourts and TV images of the country at a near standstill had the Labour Cabinet panicking even more than the motorists. Yet the Coalition gave no sign of having learned from that experience. When the tanker drivers first said they would take strike action, Cabinet minister Francis Maude calmly suggested that motorists should probably fill up their cars 'just in case'.

Within hours, the petrol pumps were almost dry as everyone rushed out to panic-buy. The government looked into the abyss and retreated; the 3p rise in fuel duty was unceremoniously dumped. It was a humiliating week for the Coalition: first exposed as out of touch and then as ineffective. The mortification was felt just as deeply in the Lib Dem ranks because they had been obliged to give their backing to the budget. Indeed, one of George Osborne's right-hand men – they were largely men – his Lib Dem colleague Danny Alexander, the chief secretary to the Treasury, had been one of the budget's principal architects. With three years still to go before the next election, many backbench Lib Dem MPs had already begun to realize their party was on borrowed time.

There was one group of people who were riding out the recession rather more comfortably than most: the bankers. The Northern Rock Building Society had been nationalized by the Labour government in 2008 at a cost to the country of about £30 billion. The failure of the Royal Bank of Scotland had cost the country another £46 billion. Lloyds TSB had been bailed out with £27 billion of taxpayers' money. In total, the 2008 bank-rescue package cost the British government £500 billion in loans and guarantees; that didn't turn out to be quite enough, though, and the government gave another £50 billion to the banks the following year.

Gratitude for not losing their jobs was never likely, but a little contrition from the bankers might have been in order. While the UK government – and other governments elsewhere around the world – hadn't gone out of their way to stop banks selling sub-prime loans to fuel a property boom, it had been the bankers themselves who had knowingly brought many of the world's economies to the point of collapse, suspecting, quite rightly, that they couldn't be allowed to go bankrupt when things inevitably went wrong. Sure, there had been one or two high-profile casualties – such as Sir Fred Goodwin, aka Fred the Shred, the RBS chief executive – to show that justice was being done – though as Goodwin left with a £700,000-a-year pension he was well compensated for failure – but for the most part, to the naked eye, it looked like business as usual.

Or non-business as usual. One of the reasons for the government bail-out of the banks had been the need to keep lines of credit open for small and medium-sized businesses; if these failed because they were unable to secure credit either to expand or ease cash-flow problems, then the economy would get worse rather than better. The banks had indicated that they understood the severity of the problem and the necessity to keep lending, but there was little sign of them acting on this under either Labour or the Coalition. The most visible sign of activity was the bankers' continued willingness to pay themselves large bonuses. This came to a head in early 2012 when it was revealed that Stephen Hester, the chief executive who had been brought in to replace Fred Goodwin, had been awarded a bonus of nearly £1 million. Even for Cameron and Osborne, this was a bit much:

Cameron: I suppose it's about time we sorted out these bankers' bonuses.
Osborne: Why? Why can't we just carry on as we have been? You know how twitchy the City gets if we try to interfere.
Cameron: I know. And for the most part I agree. Generally I'm all in favour of saying you'll do something and not doing it, because that shows we're a government that isn't prepared to ignore the tough situations. But this time we've got the whole country moaning about it.
Osborne: How about we just say no one should get more than a mill?
Cameron: That sounds about right. It should stop most of

the criticism. After all, it's hardly worth getting out of bed for that amount.

RBS: One million? That's a bloody insult. How are we going to look our mates in the eye? We'll look like an impoverished third-world institution that's going down the tubes if we're only giving six-figure bonuses.

Cameron: We all have to make sacrifices these days.

RBS: Oh, all right then. We'll just give Stephen Hester £960K.

Everyone: Let's get this straight. We own the bank, you've laid off hundreds of workers, the bank is still worth half what we paid for it and you need a million on top of your basic £1.2 million salary or you'll down tools?

Hester: It's because I'm worth it.

Cameron: Obviously it's with deep regret that we had to give Stephen his bung, but it was out of our hands.

Hester: Sod it, Cameron. I'll bloody well let my kids starve to save your skin. But you owe me.

Cameron: Don't worry, old bean. You'll still make loads from the other incentive schemes in your contract . . .

Hester eventually announced that he would refuse his bonus as a gesture that he understood people's anger with the banks. Though it appeared less of a voluntary gesture and more one he was strong-armed into making. There certainly weren't that many signs that the banking industry was going through a prolonged period of self-reflection: quite the reverse, as it soon became clear the banks were up to their necks in all kinds of trading illegalities. First came the Libor scandal, in which banks were fixing the rate of interest they were paying each other; then came the Forex scandal, in which foreign-exchange dealers had been fixing rates; finally came the exposure of their manipulation of stock exchanges through high-frequency trading.

It began to look as if there wasn't a single area of the financial-services sector that wasn't corrupt. When each scandal was exposed, the banks were at pains to make clear that only a few of their employees had been involved and that they were profoundly shocked and disgusted; but nevertheless the impression the banks were giving was that they weren't trying that hard to regulate their staff because they were making so much money from their illegal activities.

Even in early 2014, there were few signs of the banks showing any genuine remorse for the catastrophe they had caused to so many people. Nor many that the Coalition was prepared to get that tough with the City. Old habits die hard. By any standards, Barclays Bank had a bad year in 2013. Its profits were down by 32 per cent; it had been shamed in the Libor-rigging scandal; it had been forced into a £6 billion rights issue; and its share price had fallen sharply. How had Barclays responded? By paying its staff more in bonuses than it had to shareholders in dividends.

There were several shareholders at the Annual General Meeting that took place in the Royal Festival Hall on London's South Bank who weren't too happy about this. The fifteen directors of Barclays plc who were lined up on stage, like a Soviet Politburo photo from the 1970s, were unmoved. What everyone had to understand, said bank chairman Sir David Walker, a man with a voice so posh as to be almost unintelligible to normal ears, was that if these bankers weren't paid their bonuses, they would up sticks and leave to work for someone else. And then where would

Barclays be? 'Less in debt' wasn't an acceptable answer.

The head of the Barclays remuneration committee, Sir John Sunderland, was more combative. If anybody bothered to read the accounts properly, he insisted, then they would see that bonuses were actually substantially down on last year. How come? It was like this. Last year everyone would have got a great deal more than they did this year had they not had a large part of it deducted as a fine for Libor rigging. So if you just looked at the top-line figure the bankers would have got if they hadn't been caught acting illegally, then you could see that they were actually getting less this year. Only a banker could have come up with that. It wasn't an answer that impressed the shareholders at the AGM, but then the directors weren't really worried about them. The vast majority of the votes to reappoint the directors were in the hands of the large institutional investors, many of whom the board knew personally; these were all largely supportive of the board and had long since been counted. Anyone who thinks the trade-union block vote is undemocratic has never been to an AGM.

For three and a half years of Coalition government, it had seemed as if George Osborne was as out of touch as the bankers. Almost every economic report from recognized bodies, such as the Organization for Economic Cooperation and Development, suggested he had mishandled the economy. Nobel Prize-winning economists said Osborne had got it wrong. The ratings agency Moody's downgraded the UK's credit rating from the top AAA band for the first time since 1978. Just about the only person who was insistent he had got it right was Osborne himself.

Then in July 2013 the rather brittle Mervyn King retired after ten years as governor of the Bank of England and was replaced by the Canadian Mark Carney, who sounded as if he was more at home chilling on a snowboard than behind a desk in Threadneedle Street. Every sentence he spoke was delivered so slowly and so quietly in his Valium monotone that it was often a race between Carney and his listeners to see who would nod off first. If you paid very close attention you could hear him call his colleagues 'Dude'. Almost immediately the first positive noises to come from outside the chancellor's office began to be heard. The UK economy was growing faster than expected, faster than nearly any other European economy. Jobs were being created and more people were in work.

The upturn in the British economy at the same time as the arrival of a new Bank of England governor was entirely coincidental. If Mervyn King had had any idea that the good times were just around the corner he would have mentioned it in one of his farewell speeches and tried to claim some credit. But King's exit did look symbolic. Out with the old, in with the new. And Osborne was quick to trumpet his genius: 'There is still pain to come – there always is – but a corner has been turned and thanks to me, George, the good times will roll again.'

Just how much of a corner had been turned was a matter of debate. Many on the left argued the recovery was a bubble fuelled by credit-card spending and a property boom. Since 2009, the Bank of England's lending rate had been fixed at 0.5 per cent. This had the double impact of making credit cheap and saving pointless. Why bother to keep your money in the bank earning 1 per cent a year when inflation was running at about 3 per cent and in real terms you were losing money? It made sense to spend whatever cash you had. This was great news for the economy in the short term; consumer confidence is key to a recovery. Whether the long-term consequences of a spending boom with no safety net would be quite so beneficial was more uncertain, but no one at the Treasury was too worried about them. Long-term consequences are, by definition, always hard to define and, more importantly, would happen after the next election.

Governments always say we need to be careful about property bubbles, but history suggests they are usually very grateful for them. Almost every successful government – for successful read 'considered economically competent in the opinion polls' – has benefited from a bubble. It's the easiest way for a country to conjure up an illusion of wealth creation. Labour had its bubble during the first half of the 2000s and now the Coalition had theirs, caused largely by a shortage of properties in prime locations and a lack of any other realistic investment opportunities. The government did its bit to fuel the bubble with its 'Help to Buy' initiative to get people on to the housing ladder – not so much by increasing demand for houses as by raising people's expectations that home-ownership was the prime model of financial security for families. That every bubble is invariably followed by a crash was conveniently forgotten.

Osborne's recovery had other key fault-lines. The property bubble was not felt equally throughout the country. In London and the south, prices were rising far more quickly than elsewhere; many London families were earning more from the appreciation in the value of their homes than they were in salaries. Similarly, most of the well-paid jobs were being created in London and the south, which virtually excluded anyone from outside this area from applying for them, as they would not be able to afford the costs of re-location and housing. Inequality was felt elsewhere in the recovery. While the government talked up the creation of two million new jobs since it took office, it didn't specify how many of these were low paid or with zero-hours contracts. Details, details. The reality was that, by all measures, Britain was a more divided country in 2014 than it had been three years earlier. Inequality was growing. If the Tories had been in power on their own, this was a recovery the Lib Dems would have condemned. Instead, they were forced to talk it up in a bid to get some of the credit for it.

Labour struggled to get across its message that the recovery was at best uneven. Ed Miliband talked frequently about there being a cost-of-living crisis for most families – whatever recovery was going on was one that was making most people progressively a little bit more broke year on year – but his weirdly automaton-like voice was easy to ignore. He also found himself in the classic Catch-22 of all opposition leaders: good news for the government and the country is a mixed blessing. More than half the two million jobs that had been created may have been low paid or with zero-hours contracts, but they were still jobs that people had taken. Talking down good economic data never plays well for an opposition leader as it looks negative and unpatriotic; but, equally, Miliband wasn't keen to credit the government with any success. So his default position in the middle of 2014 became to remain ever more silent and to wait and pray that things got worse before the election.

The only person who might have been asking Osborne

the really tricky, existential economic questions was David Cameron:

Cameron: Just between you and me, George, did you really think you were going to turn the economy around?
Osborne: What do you mean?
Cameron: You know . . . We had all those heavyweight economists telling us we'd got it wrong and that our economic plan was prolonging the recession. I'm your biggest fan, but even I started to doubt you. I backed you in public, of course, but I don't mind telling you I had a few sleepless nights.
Osborne: I never doubted myself for a second.
Cameron: You're kidding . . .
Osborne: Of course I am, you muppet. There were a couple of years when I wondered why I had ever wanted this job in the first place. I didn't have much more of a clue about the right way to fix the economy than anyone else. All I knew was that we had to have a plan and stick with it, because changing course halfway through looks stupid.
Cameron: So what you're saying . . .
Osborne: What I'm saying is we got a bit lucky. I had it figured that if every major Western economy stayed in recession then we would too and that if there was a global upturn we'd probably be part of it. These things tend to be cyclical. But as for a cunning master plan, forget it. Look, it's possible the measures we took brought us out of recession faster than we otherwise might have managed, and . . .
Cameron: And?
Osborne: . . . and it's possible they actually prolonged the recession and we made millions of people suffer unnecessarily.

I just don't know. But these questions don't matter any more. History is written by the winners, and we've won. So we're right.

Cameron: Amazing.

With a recovery credible enough to sell to the country, Osborne's main economic plan was to keep everything ticking over. Elections are often won or lost on the performance of the economy and all the chancellor needed to do was to keep all the balls in the air for another year. In his penultimate budget before the election, the one that would set the tone for the coming campaign, Osborne had one last, give-away surprise. Pensions were going to be changed: no longer would people be forced to take an annuity on retirement. Instead they could take their whole pension pot as a lump sum and spend it how they liked.

The pension change was an unashamed appeal to the older voters who might well determine the outcome of the next election. It was a measure that said, 'We trust you, old people. We think you are grown up enough to handle your own money.' It was a classic small-state Tory policy that resonated with voters from all parties who were fed up with being sold bad annuity deals by the cartel of pension providers.

It was also a measure laden with risk. What if people weren't quite so responsible with their money as Osborne trusted them to be? What if they spent all their money in five years? What if they planned to live till eighty-five and ended up living a further ten years? Then the state that could already scarcely afford to provide for an ageing population would come under yet more pressure. More and more old people could be living in poverty. But these were risks that came with one huge advantage: they wouldn't have to be faced for another ten years. They were problems for another government at another time. Osborne's focus was much narrower: winning the election for the Conservatives in May 2015.

Chapter 7

All the Right Friends in All the Wrong Places

IT WASN'T JUST GEORGE OSBORNE'S ECONOMIC JUDGEMENT THAT came under scrutiny in the early days of the Coalition; it was also his political judgement. He had been a key figure in persuading David Cameron to appoint the former editor of the *News of the World*, Andy Coulson, as the Conservative party's director of communications back in 2007. Osborne had allegedly been impressed – not to say relieved – with the way the *News of the World*, on Coulson's watch, had reported a story involving Osborne – before his election to the House of Commons – a dominatrix and a pile of white powder. The right-wing tabloid paper, owned by Rupert Murdoch, had been unusually restrained in its coverage:

Hack: Hey, boss! I've got this great story. A prostitute is claiming she used to take cocaine with George Osborne in the early 1990s. She's even got some old photos.
Coulson: I'm not sure that's really for us . . .
Hack: What do you mean, boss? It's got everything. Politicians, hookers and drugs. It's our perfect storm!
Coulson: I'm still not quite feeling it. We could maybe do it

as a small, inside story. But we don't have a lot to stand it up . . .

Hack: Since when has that stopped us?

Coulson: I just think that this time we should show a bit of compassion. Maybe Osborne did take some coke and hang out with the dominatrix. Well, good luck to him. He was only young at the time and we've all done silly things when we were young. It would just be spiteful to ruin the career of an up-and-coming politician who could become the next chancellor of the exchequer.

Hack: Put like that, boss, I can understand where you're coming from. Shall I look for a good-news story about a woman with cancer who is raising money to save her hospital instead?

Coulson: Fuck off. You having a laugh? We've got pages to fill. Now go and find me a Premiership footballer who is out dogging and two-timing his WAG.

The suspicion remained that the *News of the World* might not have been quite so muted in its coverage if the story had involved a senior Labour politician, but Coulson's actions had marked him out as a possible future party spin doctor. He was well connected to the Murdoch empire, and having the News International papers (the *Sun*, the *News of the World*, *The Times* and the *Sunday Times*) on side had been a preoccupation of every political party for more than twenty years. Coulson had demonstrated an equal talent for keeping dangerous stories out of the press as getting good ones in it.

Spin doctors haven't enjoyed the best of reputations since Alastair Campbell laboured under the impression that he was actually a member of Tony Blair's Cabinet rather than an apparatchik tasked with communicating its policies. He inevitably ended up becoming the story he was trying to kill and he had to go. Jo Moore, a spin doctor in the Department for Transport, was forced to resign after sending out an email on the day of the 9/11 attacks on the USA in 2001 that said, 'It is now a very good day to get out anything we want to bury.' Gordon Brown's special adviser, Damian McBride, had come to a similar end in 2009 after being caught establishing a website dedicated to implicating Tory politicians in fictitious sex scandals.

Yet even by the debased standards of 2007, when it was taken as read that spin doctors were politicians manqué, Coulson's appointment was controversial. Six months before he joined Cameron's team, he had resigned from the *News of the World* after its royal editor, Clive Goodman, and a private investigator, Glenn Mulcaire, who was paid by the paper, were both jailed for phone-hacking. Coulson had always maintained this was a one-off instance of illegality of which he had no knowledge and that he had resigned purely as a matter of principle.

This always seemed unlikely. Rumours of phone-hacking at many newspapers – not just the *News of the World* – had been circulating for years and the idea that they all stemmed from this one, isolated incident was far-fetched. At the very least, David Cameron's political antennae should have been twitching during Coulson's interview for the job of Conservative party director of communications. Cameron has always maintained that he asked Coulson if he knew of any other cases of phone-hacking at the *News of the World* while he was in charge and that Coulson said 'No', and that was an end of it. How can that interview have gone?

Cameron: I'm sorry to ask you this, Andy, but I do rather have to, you know. That phone-hacking business. It was a one-off, wasn't it?

Coulson: Absolutely, Dave. On my life. I would never let anything like that happen on my watch.

Cameron: Quite right. And it must have been quite hard for you to keep tabs on everything that was going on.

Coulson: Tell me about it, Dave. But you know how it was at the *News of the Screws*. We were a totally laid-back organization. Rupert liked to give me my head and let me put in whatever I thought fit, and I liked to do the same with my staff.

Cameron: I totally get it. Rupert is such a gentle sweetheart.

Coulson: That's right. You've got to give people their heads and trust them, haven't you, Dave? You can't go micro-managing people and shouting at them that they will be sacked if they don't come up with better stories.

Cameron: Well, that's a tremendous relief. It's just how I want the Tory party operation to be run. So you can promise me that there aren't any other phone-hacking scandals to come out? That would be terribly embarrassing.

Coulson: You have my word as a former tabloid editor, Dave.

Cameron: Well, a chap can't ask for any more than that. Welcome to the Tory party, Andy.

Even without the phone-hacking blemish, Coulson was a risky appointment for Cameron. After their bruising experience of Alastair Campbell, the public was understandably suspicious of senior tabloid journalists getting close to government: so Coulson was always likely to attract more scrutiny than someone less high profile. What's more, while the electorate may have become more apathetic about tribal party politics, it had become a great deal more sophisticated in its understanding of the way politics was enacted. People had developed a gut feel for knowing when they were being lied to and when politicians were trying to gloss over their shortcomings.

For Cameron, whose brief in opposition had been to make the 'Nasty Party' Conservatives electable by rebranding them as the 'Hug-a-Hoody Party', the choice of Coulson sent out the opposite message. Hugging hoodies was just not something former *News of the World* editors did. Hoodies had always been among the paper's number-one enemies. Recasting Coulson as a neo-liberal who had always been interested in social issues was going to be a tall order. But Cameron really had no choice; or rather, not appointing Coulson would have given him far more problems than rejecting him. In the run-up to a general election, Cameron needed News International on his side, which is why he also went out of his way to court his Cotswold neighbour, Rebekah Brooks – then editor of the *Sun* and former editor of the *News of the World*, and still Rupert Murdoch's closest confidante in the UK – over cosy weekend Chipping Norton-set 'kitchen suppers'.

Brooks is thought to have been as keen on Coulson's appointment as Osborne, and there is no doubting she considered her relationship with Cameron to be more than just good neighbours. In a text message to him before his speech to the Tory party conference in 2009 she wrote, 'I am so rooting for you tomorrow not just as a proud friend but because professionally we're definitely in this together!' The exclamation mark was all hers. It just so happened that Brooks and Coulson had also had a six-year love affair, between 1998 and 2004, but neither felt this was sufficiently relevant to mention to the Conservative party leader.

Coulson became more of a problem once the Tories formed a Coalition government. For the Lib Dems there was the constant embarrassment of having a man they had, in opposition, dubbed a malign influence – a Murdoch string-puller – at the heart of Number 10. For Cameron it was just as awkward that at the time when he was trying to promote the Coalition as a new moral, unpartisan brand of politics, his inner circle of friends seemed to include so many people intimately connected with News International. If he wasn't side by side with Coulson for much of the working week, he was relaxing with Rebekah Brooks and her racehorse-trainer husband, Charlie, or TV executive Elisabeth Murdoch, Rupert's daughter, and her husband Matthew Freud, a top PR man, at weekends.

It may all have been very innocent:

Rebekah: What do you think about tax credits, Dave?

Charlie: Oh, don't bother Dave about stuff like that in his time off, Bex! How about a game of tennis?

Cameron: That would be great. Care to make a four, Liz?

Elisabeth: Why not? Then we could have a nice chat about the BSkyB deal . . .

Matthew: Don't be such a killjoy. Dave and I are going to watch *Match of the Day*.

Elisabeth: You watch the BBC and you're both dead . . .

Cameron: You've got such a great sense of humour, Liz. Tell you what, let's forget the tennis and have a drink instead. We can do something more active tomorrow.

Rebekah: We could go riding, if you like.

Cameron: I'd love to, but I don't have a horse.

Rebekah: You could borrow one of ours. We've got a lovely old police horse called Raisa.

Raisa: I'm not having him on my back. Have you seen the size of him? He'll knacker me out.

Rebekah: You'll do as you're told. And keep your ears pricked for any phone calls.

Even if it was that sociable, it still didn't look that good. Friends usually spend time with one another because they share the same set of basic values. They don't need to have conversations on many subjects because everyone already knows what the others think. Friends also look out for one another. The more time Cameron spent in the company of Rupert Murdoch's closest associates, the harder it would be on a subconscious level for him to implement policies they would naturally oppose. At the very least Cameron looked naive; gullible, even. A man who couldn't quite bring himself to believe that people with vested interests might have reasons other than friendship for wanting to spend time with the prime minister.

Suspicions of naivety grew stronger when it was revealed in 2012 that Coulson had been subject to only the most basic level of security vetting when he became press secretary at Number 10. All previous press secretaries had undergone the more rigorous 'developed vetting' before they were given access to secret, classified documents. Cameron tried to pass off the anomaly as part of his chilled attitude: developed vetting was expensive and unnecessary, as Coulson wouldn't get to see any really secret information anyway. This might have been nearly credible had not Britain been facing terror threats for more than a decade, and it was not long before the head of the Civil Service, Sir Jeremy Heywood, changed his mind about Coulson's status and in November 2010 decided to put him through the more rigorous procedure. This process was still incomplete when Coulson resigned two months later. The thought left hanging was that one reason he hadn't originally been asked to undergo developed vetting was the fear that he might fail it.

Coulson's resignation came when he had spent just eight months in the job, and it was the phone-hacking scandal that finally did for him. For years, the *Guardian* newspaper had been something of a voice in the wilderness in suggesting that Clive Goodman had not been a lone wolf at the *News of the World* and that phone-hacking had been endemic at the paper. It and the other News International titles were not the only ones interested in killing this story; virtually every other paper wanted to bury it because they didn't want to open up their own journalistic practices to public scrutiny. The *News of the World* was by no means the only phone-hacking offender.

Before the 2010 general election, the *Guardian* had run ninety-one articles about illegal activities at the *News of the World* under Coulson's editorship, but the *Guardian* had been written off by the rest of the media and many politicians as an obsessed conspiracy theorist. It could have been the plot-line from a Stieg Larsson thriller. With Coulson in Number 10, there was no question of the *Guardian* relaxing the pressure and Coulson resigned in January 2011, maintaining his innocence while saying he did not want to become a distraction to the government. Cameron stuck to his line that he had asked Coulson if the phone-hacking claims were true, had been assured they weren't and that was an end to it. Cameron had looked his friend and colleague in the eyes and seen innocence reflected back.

The tipping point came later that summer when the *Guardian* revealed that messages left on the phone of Milly Dowler, a thirteen-year-old girl who had been abducted and murdered in 2002, had been deleted by *News of the World* journalists. This turned out to be one of the few things the *Guardian* got wrong in all its many stories (a public inquiry later concluded the messages had been deleted automatically rather than deliberately), but the image of journalists hampering a police investigation for their own ends was so shocking that the mood of the public changed. Newspapers, the police – some of whom had been regularly paid by the *News of the World* for information – and politicians were forced to take phone-hacking seriously. Almost immediately a public inquiry, headed by Lord Leveson, into the culture and practices of the British press was set up and the *News of the World* was closed by News International.

In a heartbeat, Cameron switched from being Coulson's strongest advocate to becoming his sternest critic:

Coulson: Dave, it's me . . .
Cameron: Who?
Coulson: You know. Andy.
Cameron: I'm afraid I don't know an Andy.
Coulson: I was your press secretary. We had laughs together . . .

Cameron: Whoever you are, I'm afraid it's a terribly bad line. I can't hear you at all. If you'd care to phone the switchboard at Number 10 tomorrow, I'm sure my press secretary will make a note of whatever it is you want to say.

Coulson: But I *am* your press secretary. I mean, I was. I mean . . .

BBC: Good evening, Prime Minister. Would you care to comment on the allegations surrounding Andy Coulson?

Cameron: Let me make it very clear. I have always taken every allegation about phone-hacking extremely seriously. It is absolutely right for Coulson to be investigated and if he is found to be guilty he should go to prison for the rest of his life. Preferably one where he is unable to talk to anyone ever again.

BBC: And what do you think the allegations say about your judgement in appointing him?

Cameron. Good Lord, is that the time? I must dash.

Although Coulson recommended his own successor as Number 10 press secretary, Craig Oliver was a far more politically neutral appointment, having spent his career working in news for ITV, Channel 5, Channel 4 and the BBC. A full house. But even he ended up several times as the main story rather than the behind-the-scenes messenger and fixer. Three times during 2012, Oliver hit the headlines. First he had dinner with a News International lobbyist shortly after the phone-hacking story broke; then he was caught on camera shouting at a BBC journalist for his coverage of Rupert Murdoch's bid to take full control of BSkyB; and then he tried – as Maria Miller's adviser Jo Hindley had also done, in a rare moment of joined-up government – to dissuade the

Daily Telegraph from running a story about Maria Miller's expenses claims, warning the paper that, as culture secretary, she would have a role in implementing the press regulations proposed in the Leveson Report. No one could accuse him of not paying attention to detail.

There was more special-adviser trouble elsewhere. Lynton Crosby, the Australian analyst with close links to the tobacco industry who had been brought in to run the Tories' election strategy, was accused in July 2013 of having had undue influence in the government's rejection of plans to introduce plain packaging for cigarette packets. Steve Hilton, another of Cameron's SPADs, made rather different headlines. Hilton became most famous for being laid-back, environmentally friendly and riding a bike in to work – it is often suggested that he was the brains behind the shot-in-the-foot photographs of Cameron cycling to work while his ministerial car drove along behind him with his briefcase and security detail. He also made the headlines for wandering around Downing Street barefoot and for the wackiness of his blue-sky thinking – some of which might have been productive, but didn't quite send out the message that the Coalition was taking the recession seriously. In 2012, Hilton took a year's sabbatical in California, a move that suited him every bit as much as his boss.

It would be unfair to suggest that every special adviser was an accident waiting to happen; many were extremely competent. It was more that their sheer numbers made it inevitable that sooner or later things would go wrong. Although Cameron had said before he came to power that he was going to restrict the number of advisers in government, their numbers actually increased after his election. In 2010 there were sixty-five; by the following year there were ninety-seven, at a cost to the taxpayer of £7.2 million per year. The increase was partly a natural consequence of Coalition government and partly a sign of the times. Walking through the corridors of Westminster, it's almost impossible not to bump into SPADs – be they fresh-faced, swivel-eyed, unpaid interns straight out of Oxbridge, or more senior appointments. At times it feels as if they outnumber MPs by two to one.

The exact nature of the working relationship between MP and adviser is often unclear. Adam Werrity, a businessman who had been best man at the wedding of Liam Fox, the defence secretary between 2010 and October 2011, had accompanied Fox on forty of his seventy recorded official engagements. Werrity had never been security-cleared by the Ministry of Defence and Fox insisted the adviser had never worked for him in either an official or an unofficial capacity, despite the later revelation that the minister had tried to obtain public funds to bankroll him. Fox was forced to resign over the issue.

Nor are SPADs a source of potential trouble only while they are actually working for politicians. Dominic Cummings left his job as Michael Gove's closest adviser at the Department of Education in January 2014. Within six months he had created havoc, having given an interview to *The Times* in which he described David Cameron as 'bumbling' and 'a sphinx without a riddle', and Nick Clegg as a 'self-obsessed, revolting character'. Cummings also went on to attack everyone in government for not sharing Gove's vision for the education system. The interview put his former boss under the spotlight. Gove tried to distance himself from the remarks but, given the closeness of their relationship, it was impossible not to imagine that he would have shared some of Cummings's sentiments. Cummings was entirely unrepentant, resuming his attack on the prime minister within days by saying he made up policy on the hoof while 'watching Netflix with a glass of red wine in his paw'. Number 10 was ineffective, he continued, because 'senior people issue airy instructions (usually in response to a column rather than as part of a serious plan) but . . . do not know how to follow things through and ensure things get done. By the time it realizes its instructions have been ignored, months can pass.' With friends like these . . .

With so many possible disaster scenarios, you might wonder why politicians don't cut their losses by restricting the number of SPADs to a bare minimum. One reason they don't is human nature. Or, to give it its proper title, denial. Every politician knows that SPADs are a source of danger, but they all think they will be the one to avoid the pratfalls: the SPADs they have chosen will be more dependable and trustworthy than anyone else's SPADs. But there are also practical reasons. The best SPADs get things done: a minister can't hope to keep totally abreast of all areas of his brief and the SPADs are there to fill in the gaps. If a pothole suddenly appears in the B3357 Tavistock Road in Devon, a SPAD in the Department of Transport will have clocked it so that the minister can refer to it in the Commons and look on top of his or her game.

But a senior SPAD's greatest value to a minister is that he or she can be thrown to the wolves in order to save the government's skin. The lines between a ministerial and a SPAD's lapse of judgement can often be sufficiently blurred for the SPAD to take the hit. The government knows a resignation is required and it is the SPAD who walks. In June 2014 home secretary Theresa May's adviser, Fiona Cunningham, was forced to quit after posting on the Home Office website a letter from her boss that was critical of Michael Gove. May had been engaged in an ongoing row with the education secretary about who was doing more to protect the country from extremism – a row that was widely interpreted as the opening skirmishes in a leadership campaign for the Tory party if Cameron failed to win the 2015 election – and even after it hit the headlines the letter remained on the Home Office website. Initially Theresa May defended her adviser's actions, but when the heat was turned up by Downing Street after the story had remained front-page news for three days, Cunningham left the Home Office. Thus saving May from needing to do so. This led to a tricky session in the Commons for the home secretary:

Labour: So when did you insist the letter was removed from the Home Office website?
May: Immediately.
Labour: But it remained on view for three days.
May: As I said, I took it down immediately.

Theresa Time, it turned out, wasn't the same as British Summer Time. 'Immediately' for the home secretary meant three days. No one saw fit to ask her what instructions she gave her staff if something needed to be done within a few minutes rather than a few days. Really immediately? Super-immediately? But this was an embarrassment Theresa May could live with. Unlike Fiona Cunningham, she still had her job.

In 1962 the prime minister, Harold Macmillan, sacked seven members of his Cabinet in a reshuffle that became known as 'the Night of the Long Knives'. Remarking on this, the Liberal MP (and future leader of his party) Jeremy Thorpe famously misquoted from the Bible by saying, 'Greater love hath no man than this, that he lay down his friends for his life.' Over the course of more than fifty years, the idea of personal sacrifice in politics has been extended from Cabinet and parliamentary colleagues to special advisers.

Chapter 8

He Ain't Heavy, He's My Brother

WHILE THE COALITION ENJOYED THE HONEYMOON PERIOD OF ITS first few months in government, the Labour party went through a summer of intense soul-searching and introspection. How had the New Labour project gone so badly wrong? Who was to blame? Back in 1997, when Tony Blair won his first election, it had seemed genuinely possible that the Tories might be out of power for a generation. New Labour's centre-left, socialist-lite land-grab had handed them a majority of 179, leaving the Conservatives with just 165 MPs. Now, in 2010, Labour was back in opposition.

Thirteen years in power may have been a decent run for any party by the standards of British political history, but there still needed to be a post-mortem. Often in politics it's the events that a government doesn't foresee, rather than the policies it introduces for those it does, that bring it down. That was partially true for Labour. Like both the Tories and the Lib Dems, Labour had failed to predict the global financial crisis and had paid the price. But there were plenty of signs that the voters were becoming fed up with Labour even before the crash. The party would have faced an uphill battle to win a fourth term, regardless.

It was a time of reflection and recrimination they would have preferred to conduct behind closed doors. That wasn't possible, as Gordon Brown had resigned as party leader after the election and Labour had announced it would elect his successor at its party conference in September. The deputy leader, Harriet Harman, stood in as temporary leader, but Labour's main preoccupation during the interregnum was not fighting the Coalition but preventing the party from fighting itself as several candidates put their names forward for election.

Labour's problem was choosing someone who was both a senior figure within the party and not too toxic to the voters. This was easier said than done, as years of in-fighting between the Blairite and the Brownite factions, each blaming the other for whatever had gone wrong, had taken their toll. Most senior figures were clearly identified as being firmly in one camp or the other, and as far as the electorate was concerned it didn't really matter which. The Blairites were still held responsible for not telling the truth about the Iraq War and the Brownites got the flak for the state of the economy. It was a lose–lose situation.

Throughout the leadership campaign the two clear front-runners were David Miliband and Ed Balls. Although Miliband had been foreign secretary in Brown's government, he was very much still seen as a Blair man from the right wing of the party; Balls's loyalties were held to lie in the opposite camp, as he had worked at the Treasury when Brown was chancellor.

Of the two, Miliband was always ahead. Not so much because Labour was now more forgiving of the Blairites, but because he looked like a possible prime minister. He wasn't without his faults – being photographed with a banana didn't help his reputation for being a bit disconnected and weird – but he had been widely tipped as a possible future Labour leader ever since he was elected to parliament in 2001. He spoke like a possible statesman; his father was the well-known and respected left-wing academic Ralph Miliband; and the leadership was in some ways his birthright. Balls, meanwhile, was less composed. He wasn't a polished speaker; his appearance was a bit dishevelled; and while he looked a bit more fun than Miliband, he wasn't necessarily the sort of person you would want running the country.

Come the party conference in September, Labour duly elected David Miliband's brother, Ed, as its leader. After Ed Balls had been knocked out in the penultimate round of voting, Ed and David Miliband had gone into a head-to-head elimination contest and, although David got a considerably larger percentage of the votes of Labour MPs, MEPs and party members, Ed sneaked home thanks to the trade-union votes. It wasn't entirely clear if the trade unions were endorsing Ed or punishing David for having supported Tony Blair's efforts to limit their powers; fifty–fifty probably.

As the result was called, there were three simultaneous responses:

David Miliband: What the hell?
Ed Miliband: What the hell?
Everyone else: What the hell?

Quickly followed by:

David Miliband: You've elected the wrong brother . . .
Ed Miliband: You've elected the wrong brother . . .
Labour party: We've elected the wrong brother.

David Miliband's look of bewildered dismay was matched by his brother's bewildered surprise. This was an election Ed wasn't meant to win. He was seen as the quieter, more human, less successful brother, who had entered parliament four years later than David and had only been minister for energy and climate change. His candidacy had been inspired more by a desire to show he had ambitions – a marker for the future – than by any genuine expectation of winning. David could not contain his disappointment:

Ed: I know it's come as a shock to both of us, but you could at least try to look as if you're a little bit pleased for me.
David: Shan't.
Ed: If not for me, then for the party. We have to show we're united.
David: You should have thought of that before you stood against me.
Ed: If I could turn back the clock, I would. Believe me. But we can't, so we have to make the best of it.
David: I'm not listening.
Ed: How about you join my Shadow Cabinet? You can take your pick. Chancellor, home secretary . . .
David: Let me think about it. There. I've thought about it.
Ed: And . . . ?
David: You know what? I'll pass.
Ed: Please. It'll look weird without you. Besides, if I screw up—

David: *When* you screw up . . .
Ed: —you'll be in pole position to be leader after me.
David: And get your sloppy seconds? Thanks, but no thanks.
Ed: So what will you do?
David: Return to being a backbench MP.
Ed: But you will hate that . . .
David: Yup. But so will you.

Within a year, David Miliband had picked up a second job working for an international foreign-policy think tank; within three he had left parliament for good to run a US humanitarian aid charity, International Rescue. The charity may have begun at home with a salary of £300,000, but its equal attraction was the distance it put between him and Ed. Despite several contrived photo opportunities designed to show that the brothers had buried the hatchet, their relationship was never as close as it had been before the leadership election. David couldn't cope with either what he saw as the humiliation of coming second or the feeling that he had been betrayed by his brother.

Ed Miliband found it hard to shrug off the perception that he was a ruthless, fratricidal bastard who had stabbed his brother in the front. It wasn't fair, but it stuck anyway. Ed had been no more swivel-eyed in standing against David than David had been in standing against Ed, and if David had won there wouldn't have been an outcry. There was no political law of primogeniture that stated Ed was obliged to give his elder brother first crack at the leadership. The image of treachery stemmed mainly from the sense of surprise that he had won, which made it feel as if his victory must have been underhand and later became a convenient shorthand for the Tories to portray Labour as inherently untrustworthy.

David Miliband's departure from front-line politics wasn't immediately felt at a policy level: six months into the Coalition, Labour didn't particularly need any policies. What it needed was someone who could successfully challenge the government. Someone with the proven big-stage presence of David. Much as many on the left of the party had disliked David for being too closely associated with Blair, they had grudgingly had to admit he was good in the House of Commons. Labour wanted someone who could go *mano a mano* with David Cameron during the weekly Wednesday thirty minutes of Prime Minister's Questions. Someone who would give the Conservative leader a sleepless Tuesday night; possibly even a sleepless Wednesday night as well.

What Labour got was Ed. It soon became clear that, though Ed had seemed the more natural of the two brothers when the spotlight hadn't been on him, once he became leader of the opposition he gave every sign of being just as socially awkward. But without the compensatory self-confidence that had made David an effective political operator. In an ideal world, this wouldn't have mattered; politics ought to be about policy rather than personality. But it seldom is, and right from the start Labour voters struggled to connect with Ed. They found his manner and adenoidal delivery off-putting. He looked like a man who would hyper-ventilate at the idea of stepping outside a two-mile radius of his North London home. In reality, David Cameron had no more experience of dealing with ordinary people than Ed, but the prime minister did have the necessary *noblesse oblige* to give the impression of having the common touch.

It wasn't long before the Labour high command took Ed

in hand. First they tried to give him lessons in spontaneity –
a doomed project from the off:

Labour image consultant: OK, Ed. Pretend that I am an
ordinary working-class person from Rochdale who you've
just met in Morrison's.
Miliband: What's that?
Labour image consultant: A supermarket.
Miliband: Sure. Yup. I remember that now.
Labour image consultant: So approach me and start a
spontaneous conversation.
Miliband: Yeah. Er, hello.
Labour image consultant: Can you believe the price of a loaf
of bread these days?
Miliband: Er, not really. I think it's about £2.50 for an olive
ciabatta in the artisan bakery near us.
Labour image consultant: Whoa! We're going to have to
rethink this, Ed. Be more natural. And spontaneous.
Miliband: Er, hello. Are you a Labour voter?
Labour image consultant: It's just not working, is it?
Miliband: Oh? I thought I was doing a bit better . . .

In May 2011, Miliband had surgery on his adenoids. He
said it was to stop him snoring, but it must have been in the
back of his mind that it might improve the nasal quality of
his voice. It didn't. Voters were going to have to get used to
Ed and take him as they found him. Or not. By the time the
party conference came round the following year, there were
signs that the Coalition's plans for the economy were stalling
and Labour was as ready as it would ever be for Miliband's
re-launch.

Ed 2.0 was 'One Nation Ed'. This was the message of his conference speech. Time and again, he reiterated that he believed in a One Nation Britain. He was passionate about a One Nation Britain. But though in terms of its delivery this was by far the most convincing speech he had made as leader, it wasn't at all clear what he meant by 'One Nation Labour', apart from as an echo of Disraeli's late-nineteenth-century 'One Nation Conservatism'. 'One Nation' appeared to mean everything and nothing. Who could object to the idea of the whole country uniting to solve its problems jointly? Though obviously the Welsh, Scots and Northern Irish should each have wriggle-room to give the recovery some of their own identity.

One Nation felt like a good soundbite dreamed up by some Labour party policymakers; a third way between a return to old-school socialism and a continuation of Blairite New Labour, both of which had lost favour with the party's supporters; a new kind of Blue Labour that appealed to working-class Conservative concerns on immigration, the European Union and small-state management of welfare provision. In essence, it was an annexation of many of the Tory party's ideas, repackaged in a way that made them look just Labour enough to be, if not attractive, then sufficiently convincing to its supporters.

After the conference speech, Labour spin doctors promised that Miliband would flesh out his One Nation message with concrete policy proposals over the coming months. The speech had merely been an hour-long declaration of Ed's vision. It was hardly on a par with Martin Luther King's 'I have a dream', but it was a marked improvement on anything Miliband had ever said before, so many Labour supporters were prepared to give him the benefit of the doubt. They waited for the word to be made flesh. And waited. And waited. Yet the One Nation policy announcements never really materialized. Over the next few months, One Nation got mentioned in speeches from time to time, but never in a way that gave it any more depth. Within a year it was barely mentioned again. The end of Ed 2.0.

One Nation was the closest Miliband was to come to expressing his vision of Britain's future. Ed's next image re-launch, Ed 3.0, was as the pragmatist, contenting himself with criticizing the Coalition's failures and limitations – there were plenty of both – but not offering any real alternatives other than to say he would do things a bit differently. Like the Coalition, Labour would still reduce public spending, but maybe not by quite as much and perhaps in ways that wouldn't affect poor people quite so badly. Like the Coalition, it understood that the health service needed reform, but not the wholesale privatization on which the current government was hell-bent. On education, Labour did endless reverse-ferrets. First it was opposed to free schools, then it was in favour in a limited kind of way, then it wasn't again, and then it was. Or that's the way it felt.

Labour seldom adopted unorthodox positions; rather it just looked a bit tired and uninspired, qualities that are usually the hallmark of a struggling mid-term government rather than a mid-term opposition. Miliband's Labour gave the impression that its sole strategy was to wait passively for the Coalition to make a catastrophic mistake while ensuring it kept its own to a minimum. The battle was to see who blinked first.

Labour did make a few errors. On one occasion the

shadow chancellor, Ed Balls, let slip that Labour would increase the top rate of tax to 50p:

Miliband: You said what?
Balls: That we would increase the top rate of tax.
Miliband: But you can't say that.
Balls: Why not? It was basically your idea. You told me that public services need more money and the rich can afford to give a bit more.
Miliband: I know I said that to you, but we can't say it in public. The rich don't like it.
Balls: But what about the poor?
Miliband: They don't matter. We need the rich on our side. Nobody ever won a general election by promising to put up taxes. If we start saying we will, we'll have all the right-wing media coming out against us.
Balls: So we have to pretend there's already more than enough money in the kitty to pay for all our funding promises and all that's required is just a few sensible efficiency measures to make sure there's no waste.
Miliband: That's what our £10,000-per-day focus group and image consultants keep telling me.
Balls: Fair enough.

Miliband's bet – hope, even – was that some unforeseen event would come along to push the Coalition into free-fall and make any minor slips on Labour's part look insignificant. As a strategy, this has some merit; but voters recognized it for what it was – reactive. This in turn was reflected in opinion polls that consistently showed Labour to be ahead of the Conservatives, but not by the amount it should have been given the difficulties the Coalition was facing, nor by enough to guarantee a return to government at the next election. More tellingly still, Miliband's personal ratings were much, much lower than Cameron's. Voters may not have been overwhelmed by the success of the Coalition, but they still thought Cameron was a better man to lead the country. Go figure, as the Americans say.

The Labour grandees and backbenchers did go figure. In mid-2013 the briefings against Miliband started. First came David Blunkett, a former home secretary under Tony Blair, saying Miliband risked turning the party into a mere repository for grievance. Then John Prescott, the former deputy prime minister, weighed in by declaring Labour had 'massively failed' to get its message across in opposition. To cap it all, Gordon Brown's ex-spin doctor, Damian McBride, used the Labour party conference as a platform to launch his memoirs, in which he laid bare the rivalries between Brown and Blair and implicated Miliband in briefing against his opponents. The Labour party was doing the Conservatives' job for them.

Some senior Labour figures made a point of calling for party loyalty, but in some ways that only made the problem worse by drawing attention to it. There was no getting away from the fact that most people found Miliband a distant, odd and uninspiring figure, and the harder he tried not to be, the more distant, odd and uninspiring he appeared. The 2014 European and local elections told the familiar story of Labour's under-performance: an improvement on the previous, disastrous results, but not as great as was either hoped for or expected.

Then the sniping resumed in earnest. In one twenty-four-hour period Miliband had Lord Mandelson rubbishing him on *Newsnight* and Alan Johnson, his former shadow chancellor, saying he had problems with his 'geek' image and that his brother would probably have been a better leader. The only thing keeping Miliband vaguely upright at this point was the ferocity of the simultaneous stabs to his front and back. He tried to make light of it, but the strain showed in his eyes. At the launch of new policy proposals to cut benefits for teenagers unless they were in training, Miliband looked like the walking dead. He said he was relishing the prospect of the next ten months before the election, but it didn't appear that way.

Miliband was stuck in the ultimate Catch-22. If he said nothing, his ratings fell. If he said something, his ratings fell. If he died, his ratings would probably also fall. However, the Labour party was in a parallel double-bind. Miliband might not be a good party leader, but getting rid of him so soon before an election would look like panic. Besides which, there weren't any obvious candidates to replace him. Labour did have one thing going for it, though. The electoral arithmetic. Given the first-past-the-post electoral system and constituency boundaries that worked in Labour's favour, it was quite possible that Miliband's and Labour's current poll ratings would be enough to ensure they were the largest party after the next election. It wouldn't be the triumphant march to victory that they would have liked. But sometimes it's OK to settle for just staggering across the line with your nose in front.

Chapter 9

Down, Down, Deeper and Down

FOR THE FIRST FEW MONTHS OF THE COALITION, DAVID Cameron and Nick Clegg appeared as equals in public. Confident, happy and relaxed in each other's company, it frequently felt as if the prime minister and the deputy prime minister were blood brothers. The politics were personal. The Coalition wasn't the grubby compromise of two parties desperate for a shot at power; it was a genuine meeting of minds between two leaders with shared beliefs and values. Men who could roll up their sleeves together – Clegg had become just as keen on rolling up his sleeves as Cameron – to solve the country's problems and then relax together over a game of tennis and a few glasses of Sauvignon Blanc. British politics had its first cross-party love affair between two leaders.

Cameron, though, never really shared this vision. It suited him to be regarded as a modern, flexible, listening leader, and he did quite enjoy Clegg's company, but equality was never on offer. He was the number one and Clegg the number two. The Conservative party still blamed him for not securing an outright majority and he couldn't afford to give too much away. The government may have been a coalition in name, but it needed to be fundamentally Conservative in nature if there weren't to be loud grumbles from his backbenchers.

In his heart, Clegg must have been aware of this. He had been involved in politics for long enough to know how things worked; and yet initially he gave the impression of believing that the Coalition really was different and that the Lib Dems would have an equal voice. Maybe he needed to believe that in order to do the deal; maybe he had been seduced by being the first leader to take the Lib Dems into any form of power and his judgement was clouded by that; maybe being in government was so thrilling and intoxicating that he just didn't care. Whichever it was, it was not long before hubris cut in.

There were a few early-warning signs of the problems the Lib Dems would face in power. Before the election, Lib Dem deputy leader and Treasury spokesman Vince Cable had been the scourge of the bankers. While he hadn't always been wholly consistent in his policy ideas – in 2008 he was against pumping government money into the economy; by the following year he was in favour of quantitative easing – he had always been extremely critical of the bonus culture in the City. After the election and his promotion to business secretary, Cable became more measured about the need to regulate financial institutions. At the end of 2010, undercover reporters from the *Daily Telegraph* recorded him during a meeting in his constituency airing his frustration at being part of a Tory-led coalition.

The biggest image disaster for the Lib Dems came later in the same year over university tuition fees. Before the 2010 election, every single one of the fifty-seven Lib Dem MPs who were subsequently elected had signed a National Union of Students pledge to vote against plans to raise tuition fees from £3,000 to

£9,000 per year in the next parliament – a promise that had won the party the support of many students and also many Labour voters disenchanted with their own party's stance on the issue. On 9 December 2010, twenty-seven Lib Dem MPs, including Clegg and Cable, voted with the government in favour of raising tuition fees and the Bill was passed:

Clegg: Tuition fees are a bit of a tricky one for us, Dave.
Cameron: Mmm. I should imagine they are.
Clegg: Do you think you could help me out a bit here?
Cameron: How do you mean?
Clegg: We're going to look awful if we just blindly back you. So could you maybe consider a teeny-weeny compromise? How about if we reduced the fees to £8,645? Would you think about that?
Cameron: Yup, I'd think about that . . .
Clegg: Oh, thank you. Our Lib Dem supporters need to see we are getting key concessions.
Cameron: One, two, three. There. I've thought about it and the answer's no. It's still 9K.
Clegg: But everyone is going to hate us . . .
Cameron: It was bound to happen sooner or later. Best face up to it now.
Clegg: I thought we were equals.
Cameron: Whoever gave you that idea?
Clegg: You did.
Cameron: You didn't actually believe any of that crap, did you . . . ? Oh! You did. How terribly sweet!
Clegg: Please. I'm begging you. Just this once. Help me out and afterwards you can do whatever you like with the Lib Dems . . .

Cameron: I already can . . .

Clegg: Tuition fees were our red-line issue. We can't be seen to be backing down on this.

Cameron: If you look really closely, that red line doesn't look quite so red. In a certain light it looks so pale it's almost pink.

Cable: So it does . . . In fact, to me it seems a bit orange.

Cameron: That's the spirit.

Clegg: Oh, all right. We'll vote for you just this once. But I want concessions.

Cameron: Sure. I'll let you stay on as deputy prime minister. How does that sound?

Clegg: Pretty good to me.

The tuition-fee U-turn destroyed the credibility of the Lib Dems in coalition for many of its supporters. The one key policy that differentiated them from Labour and the Tories, and on which everyone within the Lib Dems had been agreed, had been ditched within a year. The Lib Dems might have wrung a few minor concessions over the salary threshold at which students would have to start paying back their tuition-fee debt, but the headline increase to £9,000 per year stayed. Clegg didn't help himself by saying he should have been more careful about signing the NUS pledge rather than sticking to his principles, while Cable argued that all bets had been off the moment they didn't get an outright majority at the election, as after that the Lib Dems couldn't possibly keep all their manifesto promises.

This was a statement Cable soon came to regret, as it shone far too bright a light into the new Lib Dem mindset. For a start, it made any election promise they had ever given look meaningless. The Lib Dems had never been in with a chance of getting an outright majority at any point in their history. Did this mean that everything they had said during the election campaign amounted to no more than a collection of feel-good ideas that the party would quite like to happen? World peace? That would be nice. All unemployed people working on wind farms? That would be nice too. Most importantly, though, Cable implied that there was no issue on which the Lib Dems would stand firm. Tuition fees had been a core part of their election campaign; if that could be ditched within a year, then what *did* the party hold sacred?

Clegg tried to explain away the Lib Dem volte-face as a sign of the realpolitik of modern, grown-up coalition life. You win some, you lose some. There was some truth to this. The Coalition was about compromise; if the Lib Dems were going to vote only for those Conservative policies with which it agreed, it might as well have decided against forming a coalition and let the Tories rule as a minority government.

The difficulty for the Lib Dems was that there was a growing perception that they lost some and then they lost some more. The claims that they were smoothing off the harder edges, and that Tory policy would be a great deal nastier were the Lib Dems not in office, looked hard to justify. To all intents and purposes, the Coalition appeared indistinguishable from a Cameron-led Conservative government, because on all the important issues the Tories were getting their own way. So while Lib Dem supporters experienced the tuition-fee vote as a personal betrayal, its greater significance in political terms was in what it said about the party's place in government. Despite having five MPs in the Cabinet, any power the Lib Dems held was largely cosmetic.

For the Conservatives, the Coalition was now looking a

far better deal than it had at the beginning. They weren't even getting the flak parties usually get in government when they have to implement unpopular policies. Rather than blaming the Tories for introducing the £9,000 tuition-fee rise, all the negative focus was on the lack of Lib Dem resistance to it. The Conservatives were merely doing what they had said they would; it was the Lib Dems who had changed. They were the ones at fault. The same thing happened with other measures too. The Tories escaped some of the heat because the public blamed the Lib Dems for not keeping them more firmly in check. The Lib Dems became the Coalition scapegoat.

Even when there was nothing overtly party political in Coalition policy, the Lib Dems seemed to get the raw deal. Among its austerity measures to tackle the economic deficit, the Coalition had cut many public-sector jobs as part of its reduction in government expenditure:

Clegg: I've just realized something, Dave.
Cameron: What's that?
Clegg: All these people we are making redundant in the public sector are far more likely to be Lib Dem voters than Tories . . .
Cameron: Do you know what? I'd never really given it a moment's thought. But now you mention it, you're probably right. I don't suppose we do get many social workers voting Conservative.
Clegg: So what's actually happening is that the government is putting a disproportionately high number of possible Lib Dem voters out of work.
Cameron: When you put it like that, Nick . . . But do try

not to take it too personally. It will all come out in the wash.
Clegg: Do you think we could have a few measures to put just a few Tory voters out of work?
Cameron: I really don't think that's a very good idea. It would just look petty and vindictive, and that's not what the Coalition is about at all. Besides, all your social workers will soon find jobs in the private sector.
Clegg: Where?
Cameron: I'm not sure, precisely. But George is adamant that there are loads being created.
Clegg: I don't see them.
Cameron: Perhaps you should look a bit harder . . .
Clegg: While I have your attention, can we also chat about the fact that the people whose benefits we are cutting are far more likely to be Lib Dems than Tories?
Cameron: You don't.
Clegg: Don't what?
Cameron: Have my attention.

The number of new private-sector job opportunities did eventually grow significantly towards the beginning of 2014, but by then most of the damage had already been done to the Lib Dems. In the eyes of many, they had become the nation's punch-bag, a by-word for broken promises and political ineffectiveness. When they weren't being mugged by their Coalition partners, they were busy shooting themselves in the foot.

Electoral reform had long been a mainstay of Lib Dem policy. For good reason, too, as the British first-past-the-post electoral system clearly put them at a disadvantage against the two main parties. At the 2010 general election, the Lib

Dems won 23 per cent of the total votes, yet they won only 57 of the 650 seats in the House of Commons. Meanwhile, the Conservatives won 36 per cent of the vote and 307 seats, and Labour won 29 per cent of the vote and picked up 258 seats. Apart from it being so obviously in the self-interest of the Conservatives and Labour not to change the electoral system, the argument that both parties and many constitutional experts used to justify the retention of the first-past-the-post system was that it produced strong governments with absolute overall majorities and that reforming it would lead to a succession of the hopeless, messy coalitions that lasted barely a year and had become a feature of other European countries, notably Italy.

The 2010 election put paid to that last argument. This time the first-past-the-post system had not produced a strong government; the British electorate had specifically said it did not want to give control to just one party. It seemed as if the Lib Dems' moment had come. They didn't just have fairness on their side – no one had ever tried to claim first-past-the-post was anything but unfair – they also had the nation on their side. There had been a steady groundswell of support for electoral reform in the previous parliament as part of the process of restoring trust in political life after the MPs' expenses scandal; after the election the call for change was irresistible and the Lib Dems had made a referendum on electoral reform a non-negotiable part of the Coalition agreement.

Within a year the Lib Dems had lost the vote and the possibility of electoral reform was off the political agenda for the foreseeable future. How had they managed to play such a strong hand so badly? Had they been too naive? Or were they totally outmanoeuvred by their Conservative partners who never had any interest in reforming the system?

During the negotiation to form the Coalition, the Conservatives had agreed to hold a referendum offering a choice between the Alternative Vote (AV) or retaining the first-past-the-post system. At the time it had appeared a landmark deal between the two parties, but it gradually became clear that the Lib Dems were not entirely happy. AV was very much at the lower end of their electoral reform wish-list; an improvement on first-past-the-post in that it allowed voters to rank candidates in order of preference, but still a system designed to produce just a single winner in each constituency and therefore one that would continue to favour the two largest parties. Had AV been used in the 2010 election, the Lib Dems would have won 79 seats, a gain of just 22 over first past the post. The Conservatives would have held 281 seats and Labour 262.

The Lib Dems had always been advocates of the Single Transferable Vote – a system of proportional representation in which the percentage of votes cast for each party is more accurately reflected in the number of MPs returned to parliament by having large, multi-member constituencies. Under STV, the Lib Dems would have won 162 seats at the 2010 election, Labour 207 and the Conservatives 246 – a result that might have transformed the British political landscape for good. With 162 seats, the Lib Dems could have played a far more equal role in any coalition, and both the Tories and Labour would have had to offer them many more concessions in the negotiating process than either did. More significantly, it would have allowed the Lib Dems to form a strong coalition with Labour, the party to which they had always been ideologically far closer. Together, the Lib Dems and Labour might have kept the Conservatives in opposition indefinitely.

For just these reasons, the Conservatives had been determined to keep STV off any electoral-reform referendum agenda. What's not clear is just how hard the Lib Dems battled for it:

Clegg: We won't do any deal without electoral reform.

Cameron: We quite understand. We wouldn't expect anything else. So how about we agree on a referendum for AV in a year's time?

Clegg: We want STV.

Cameron: What's that?

Clegg: It's a multi-member constituency system.

Cameron: Gosh. That sounds awfully complicated . . .

Clegg: Well, it is a bit, but I'm sure we can explain it to the public.

Cameron: I'm not so sure. I think we should start with something a lot more straightforward. Like AV. British people hate big changes. They find it very frightening and terribly European.

Clegg: We'd still much rather have STV, Dave . . .

Cameron: Look, Nick, which part of N-O don't you get? It's AV or nothing.

Clegg: Please . . .

Cameron: Forget it, then. We'd much rather try our luck as a minority government than risk signing up to a voting system that could finish off the Conservatives.

Clegg: Then we'll have to go and chat to Labour . . .

Cameron: I don't think you will find them any more enthusiastic.

Clegg: But AV is such a rubbish system . . .

Cameron: I know. That's the beauty of it. But try and be a little more realistic. Most people haven't a clue what the difference between STV and AV is – I'm not sure I have, for that matter – and if you say you've secured a referendum on AV, everyone will think you must have been a brilliant negotiator.

Clegg: I'm still not convinced.

Cameron: Do you want to be deputy prime minister or not?

Clegg: I'm convinced.

Having forced a referendum on electoral reform, the Lib Dems failed to get behind the campaign and make the case for AV. Clegg's heart wasn't in it. He had previously dismissed AV as a 'miserable little compromise' and nothing he did or said in the run-up to the referendum indicated he had changed his mind. This was a bad tactical mistake. Having secured the best referendum he could get, he should have got behind AV and tried to sell it to the country. It might not have been exactly what he wanted, but it could have been a transitional bargaining chip from which to make the case for a better form of proportional representation later. Why bother to go to all the trouble of negotiating a referendum if he wasn't going to endorse it fully? The country noted the indifference with which all parties regarded AV and voted accordingly. On a turnout of just 42 per cent, two-thirds voted to retain the first-past-the-post system. Clegg had put back the cause of electoral reform by a generation.

Along with electoral reform and student tuition fees, a third pillar of Lib Dem policy was reform of the unelected House of Lords, the upper chamber of parliament. In May

2011, Clegg announced proposals to reduce the number of peers from about 780 – there is no fixed number – to just 300, most of whom would be elected. Within just over a year, he had to abandon these reforms as large numbers of Conservative backbenchers were opposed to them and they would never get through parliament. In retaliation, Clegg said the Lib Dems would refuse to back the Tories' Bill for constituency boundary changes. While this was potentially extremely damaging for the Tories, as the changes could have given them up to twenty extra seats at the next general election in 2015 – a huge advantage in a tight vote – the immediate effect of the Coalition fallout was felt most acutely by the Lib Dems.

If the Lib Dems couldn't impose any part of their three biggest pre-election promises on the Conservatives, then what was the point of them being in government at all? The Coalition had been sold as a coming together of equals. Or near equals. Yet it was now clear there was nothing very equal about it at all. The Tories were able to ignore or see off any Lib Dem reforms they didn't like, and all that was left for the Lib Dems was to claim they were softening Conservative policy. Telling the country 'You might not like what the Coalition is doing, but please trust us that it would be even worse if we weren't around' had become almost the Lib Dems' last selling point.

It wasn't a very effective one. Lib Dem poll ratings fell dramatically from a high of 23 per cent at the 2010 election to single figures after the vote on university tuition fees and they never really recovered. Apart from a few lone by-elections in which Lib Dem votes held up for a strong local candidate, the party continued to haemorrhage support on a national level. In the 2012 local elections, they lost more than 300 councillors, reducing the number of seats they held to the lowest in the party's history; two years later, in the 2014 local elections, they lost a further 300.

There was seemingly no bad situation that the Lib Dems couldn't make worse. In 2013, the party's chief executive, Lord Rennard, was accused by four party activists of sexual harassment. Rather than immediately initiating an inquiry to establish what had happened, the Lib Dem hierarchy gave the impression that they were trying to sweep the allegations under the carpet. Lord Rennard was an important member of the Lib Dem strategy team; to lose him would have been embarrassing, so they dithered in the hope it would all go away. It didn't, and from there on the party was on the back foot. They eventually asked Lord Rennard to apologize: he refused, before later offering an apology that sounded half-hearted.

Nor did it help when in 2013 the marital problems of Chris Huhne, the Lib Dem secretary of state for energy and climate change, ended at Southwark Crown Court with a prison sentence for perverting the course of justice. Huhne had left his wife, the economist Vicky Pryce, a few weeks after the 2010 election to live with Carina Trimingham, who had been part of his campaign team and with whom he had been having an affair. Pryce took her revenge by telling a newspaper reporter that in 2003 she had agreed to take the penalty for a speeding offence that her husband had been caught on camera committing by saying she had been the driver of the car in question. Huhne denied it vehemently, only to change his plea to guilty on the first day of the trial. It didn't take a great deal of imagination to envisage a parallel scenario in which the allegations could have been resolved at far less cost to the reputations of all involved, while also retaining some public sympathy. Instead, Huhne self-destructed on a grand scale, making not just himself but his party too look incompetent and untrustworthy.

Everything that Clegg tried in his efforts to redeem the Lib Dems' position backfired. He agreed to take part in a weekly phone-in on LBC, a London local radio station. The plan was for him to engage with listeners on a one-to-one basis and rebuild the image he had acquired for himself before the 2010 election as a politician with the common touch, who understood ordinary people's concerns. There was a time when this might have worked for Clegg, but that time had long since passed. He was seldom less than affable and chatty, but as an exercise in restoration it was a failure. If Clegg was making the case for why the Lib Dems had been so successful in Coalition, no one was hearing him. All listeners really wanted to talk about were the Lib Dems' failures and broken promises.

Not even an improving economy in 2014 helped the party. People either didn't much trust the data, or they gave all the credit to the Conservatives. The Lib Dems had become the convenient dumping ground for everything that people disliked about, or thought had gone wrong with, the Coalition. When Clegg made speeches that talked up his party's role in mending the economy and creating a fairer society, what people heard was the exact opposite:

Clegg: Perhaps some of you have wondered why the Lib Dems have not challenged the Tories over cuts in public spending. For those people, let me spell it out clearly. We have almost no say in the government's economic policy.

Worse still, were we now to tackle the government head on over the important issues, we would find ourselves even more sidelined than we are already. At its philosophical core, this party believes in freedom. The freedom to let the Tories do whatever they want and to use us as scapegoats. I'm proud of that tradition of freedom, and come the next election I want every Lib Dem candidate to be able to look voters straight in the eye and say, 'We did next to nothing to help the poorest members of the community.' We've made mistakes. I've made mistakes. But we can no longer afford to be the party that dwells on the past. If we want to avoid becoming a footnote in history, we need to move forward together with amnesia.

Clegg's loss of stature was reflected in his performance in the House of Commons. He still sat at Cameron's right-hand side during Prime Minister's Questions, but his presence was diminished. Cameron seldom acknowledged him and when he did it was only as a charitable afterthought; it felt as if Clegg was shrinking before parliament's eyes. If his rate of decline continued at a similar pace, he would soon be auditioning for comedian Rob Brydon's *Man in a Box*.

His humiliation was almost painful to watch. Politics can be a cruel business in the Commons and MPs seldom pass up the opportunity to expose each other's weaknesses. That's the way it works, and politicians have to develop a thick skin to survive; being ridiculed and attacked is a perverse sign of power, implying that you are an adversary worth taking seriously. Clegg, though, began to be killed with kindness in the Commons. The attacks on him became less frenzied and personal – more in sadness than in anger – as if there was an implicit understanding that his career was in free-fall and that to mention it too loudly or frequently would be to intrude on a personal grief.

Clegg's only possible safety net was the lack of alternative options. It was unlikely the Lib Dems would mount a campaign to remove him as leader before the 2015 election, as that would make the party look panicky; and, as much as the Tories had started to freeze the Lib Dems out of the day-to-day processes of government, they couldn't afford to do so entirely in case they needed to form another coalition in the next parliament. Even so, his long-term survival chances were poor; even if the Lib Dems were asked to form a coalition with either the Tories or Labour after the election, it was a request that would almost certainly come at the cost of his position. Clegg was a tainted brand and any new coalition would require his removal to underline that it was going to be an entirely fresh start. But a drowning man has to believe in something and there wasn't much else for Clegg to hope for.

Chapter 10

Master of Puppets

IF PHONE-HACKING ALLEGATIONS HAD LOOKED LIKE A Scandinavian *noir* thriller before the Milly Dowler tipping point, after it they resembled a Shakespearean bloodbath in which many of the leading players were stabbing anyone and everyone in order to distance themselves from the affair. 'No, they had never had anything much to do with Andy Coulson.' 'Yes, they had always had doubts about his appointment.' For weeks, politicians and prominent public figures embarked on extensive, hand-wringing soliloquies, lamenting any possible involvement of their own, combined, of course, with assertions of their absolute innocence and ignorance of everything. The final *coup de théâtre* was the arrival of King Lear himself, aka Rupert Murdoch, who flew into Britain to take personal control over, and to shore up, his media empire after the closure of the *News of the World*.

Asked what his priority was, the eighty-year-old News Corp owner gestured towards and then smiled at Rebekah Brooks, who was standing by his side. 'This one,' he said. At the time, it wasn't entirely clear if she was Goneril, Regan or Cordelia, but it later turned out not to matter much as Murdoch was as good as his word. His devotion to Brooks didn't overly impress many of the *News of the World* journalists who had lost their jobs the previous weekend for alleged offences committed on her watch as News International chief executive. Collective responsibility was not part of the News Corp management plan. Murdoch's strategy was to save Brooks; if not for the nation, then for himself. And possibly even for her husband, Charlie, though he had always seemed a minor player in Murdoch and Brooks's relationship.

It was a tricky time for all concerned. The political class had to make a public display of distancing themselves from Murdoch, Brooks and News International, but in private it was still pretty much business as usual. Coulson may have been cast adrift, but the dinners and parties went on as before, only with more effort to keep them out of the gossip columns. In July 2013 David Cameron, George Osborne and other senior Conservative politicians were guests at Matthew Freud and Elisabeth Murdoch's summer party at their home in the Cotswolds. As was Alastair Campbell, Tony Blair's former spin doctor, who had assiduously courted the Murdochs on his boss's behalf. The Murdochs had always been equal opportunities employers.

Murdoch had long been one of the shrewdest operators in the media world. In 1969 he had bought the *News of the World*, closely followed by the *Sun*. Twelve years later he bought *The Times* and the *Sunday Times*, giving him key footholds in both tabloid and broadsheet newspapers, providing him with the ideal power base to promote his business interests and his natural conservative agenda. Politicians from all parties came to fear him, believing he could make or break them. Stay onside with Murdoch and you had a far better chance of both your policies and your private life appearing in a better light: Murdoch never saw much difference between the two when politics was involved and was happy to do whatever was necessary to achieve his ends.

It became a Murdoch boast that he had never backed a loser in a general election campaign. In 1997, the *Sun* backed Labour for the first time. Tony Blair and Alastair Campbell congratulated themselves on a job well done in making Labour policies sufficiently attractive to a loyal Tory readership; others in the Labour party wondered just how much they had needed to care about Murdoch's support. The Conservatives had never had a hope of winning the 1997 election and Murdoch would always have backed Labour rather than be seen supporting a loser. Losing has never been Murdoch's strong point.

By 2010, political parties and the Murdoch empire had become so entwined that it was impossible to tell which was the parasite and which the host. Perhaps they needed each other equally. While the politicians were always keen to keep up the appearance of independence, and also of being in charge, in fact few decisions were ever taken without at least considering how Murdoch might react. If you were going to do something you thought might not greatly please him, it was important to try to mitigate the damage.

This, though, was merely the formal process of policy and decision-making. Informally, the connections were as deep, if not deeper. Over time, the two powerful elites had become friends. They may have had a few ideological differences, but there was much more that they had in common. They went to the same events, they shared the same friends, they enjoyed doing the same things. They became part of the same social eco-system, in which Rebekah Brooks letting David Cameron ride one of her old nags was not a shameless bargaining chip for power but the kindness of one friend to another. Which, in itself, it might have been. Their failure was their inability to appreciate how this might look to anyone who was not inside their bubble. One of the pleasures of friendships is the shorthand that comes with them; the things that don't need to be said because they are already understood. Implicit in every true friendship is that keeping an eye out for each other's interests is part of the deal. Trying to persuade the country that Brooks and Cameron were capable of separating a private friendship from their public interests was always going to be difficult. In public life, there are some friendships that have to be kept at arm's length.

As with so many other matters, it was Tony Blair who had muddied the waters and made life difficult for those who followed. Blair had unashamedly cosied up to Murdoch while in office and had, in 2010, become godfather to Grace, Murdoch's daughter with his third wife, Wendi Deng. There was something almost medieval in two great families making such a symbolic statement of togetherness. Had Cameron been truly interested in a new, transparent form of Rose Garden politics, he would have understood the importance of making his separation visible. He would not have employed Andy Coulson as head of Conservative communications and Number 10 press officer. Nor would he have had informal weekend supper and riding parties with Brooks. Nor, for that matter, would he have made an iffy situation look even worse with his handling of Murdoch's News Corp bid to take control of the satellite TV broadcaster BSkyB.

It had been the business secretary, Vince Cable, who had originally been in charge of determining if News Corp's bid for the remaining 61 per cent of BSkyB it did not already own contravened government guidelines on monopolies and press freedom. But after Cable had been caught out parading his machismo to two undercover women reporters from the *Daily Telegraph* by announcing he was 'declaring war on the Murdochs', his impartiality was called into question and Cameron handed the BSkyB bid over to Jeremy Hunt, the secretary of state for culture, media and sport.

Cable's indiscretions were a godsend for Cameron. Much as he might personally have liked to give Murdoch whatever he wanted, the prime minister knew he was going to have to be seen to be playing with a straightish bat. Murdoch wasn't a figure universally loved outside Chipping Norton and some kind of due process needed to be followed. Cable, though, was too straight a bat: a politician whose natural inclination would be to look for reasons to say no to the deal. Hunt was a man who could be relied on to keep his bat at more of an angle: someone, like the man from del Monte, who was predisposed to say 'Yes'. Or, in Cameron's view, was entirely neutral. It wasn't long before Hunt rejected the advice of Ofcom, the independent regulator, and decided there was no need to refer the bid to the competition authorities. In June 2011, Hunt gave his backing to the bid.

Not for the first time – and certainly not for the last – it was a special adviser who put the government's role in the spotlight, when it emerged that a News Corp lobbyist, Frederic Michel, appeared to have been getting regular briefings from inside Hunt's department about how the bid was progressing. As so often in these cases, the department investigated these leaks thoroughly and decided it had acted with the utmost integrity and that any transgressions had been those of a lone, rogue adviser, Adam Smith, who had exaggerated his influence and was acting without the minister's knowledge or approval. What didn't get answered – possibly because it didn't need to be – was how accurately Smith was reporting what was going on inside the department: special advisers are usually fairly reliable weather vanes of their master's voice. A tipping point came when Hunt was invited on to Radio 4's *Today* programme to be interviewed by Jim Naughtie:

Naughtie: It seems that News International felt they were getting reliable information about the bid from inside your department.
Hunt: That's complete nonsense.
Naughtie: But there are a great many emails suggesting otherwise.
Hunt: Ah! Those emails . . .
Naughtie: Yes, those emails.
Hunt: Yes, those emails that I had never heard about till yesterday.
Naughtie: Can you tell us a bit more about those emails?
Hunt: Umm. Let me think . . . No.
Naughtie: So you have no idea why one of your special advisers might have been in regular touch with a Murdoch lobbyist?
Hunt: None whatsoever. Wait a minute . . . Listen to that noise . . .
Naughtie: What noise?

Hunt: The sound of Adam Smith falling from a tenth-floor window. So sad. Can I go now?
Naughtie: Thank you for talking to us, Mr Cunt.

That last faux pas might have sounded like less of a Freudian slip had not another broadcaster, Andrew Marr, also referred to Jeremy Hunt as Jeremy Cunt within the hour on the same radio station. Hunt had never been the most popular of ministers at the BBC, but even so . . .

The BSkyB bid was shelved soon after the Leveson Inquiry got under way. The inquiry's main purpose was to investigate the role of the press and the police in the phone-hacking scandal, but it also turned up some intriguing glimpses into the symbiotic relationships between politicians and the Murdochs. When Rebekah Brooks found herself more firmly in the phone-hacking spotlight after the Milly Dowler revelations, she received an email from Tony Blair in which he expressed no sympathy for the victims but urged her to stay strong, take sleeping pills and set up a quasi-independent inquiry, similar to the Hutton Inquiry he had established after the Iraq War, which would throw the public a few inconsequential bones and exonerate her completely.

Cameron needed to be more circumspect: he had to be seen to be keeping his distance. It wasn't always easy, as the phone-hacking saga descended from Shakespearean tragedy and revenge into pure farce, culminating with a member of the public being assaulted by Murdoch's wife, Wendi, after he had thrown a foam pie at her husband when he appeared before a parliamentary select committee. Many of the main witnesses' appearances before Leveson were well rehearsed to give away as little information as possible, but even with expert coaching it was hard to spin much of the detail into a positive light. As well as the revelation of an email from Cameron to Brooks describing his ride on Raisa as racy, 'Fast, unpredictable and hard to control. But fun' – Raisa never did get a chance to say if she had found the experience equally enjoyable – it also turned out that he often signed off his emails to her with LOL; he stopped only when Rebekah pointed out that LOL meant 'Laugh out Loud' and not 'Lots of Love'.

Brooks's messages to Cameron were just as intimate. In one text, she said she had sobbed twice during his speech at the Tory party conference – no one else in the UK had even cried once – and that she would 'love working together'. Cameron also later sent her a message saying how sorry he was that he couldn't be more loyal to her in public while the criminal investigation into phone-hacking was ongoing. Theirs was a relationship whose boundaries were completely blurred. Many of the messages sounded more like those of a couple of teenagers than of a prime minister and the chief executive of one of the world's most powerful media organizations.

Even when the phone-hacking trial was under way and politicians might have been well advised to keep their distance from Rupert Murdoch, his attraction proved irresistible to some. Boris Johnson, London mayor and one of the foremost contenders in any future Conservative leadership contest, and Michael Gove, the then education secretary and another Tory nursing leadership hopes, both had dinners with Murdoch which they tried to keep secret. Even with the possibility that widespread criminality had been endemic in his organization and that several of his former senior employees might go to prison, Murdoch was still too important a figure for politicians to ignore. If they wanted to advance their careers, they needed his support and would go out of their way to get it.

In June 2014, the phone-hacking trial ended. Andy Coulson – along with three other senior *News of the World* journalists who had pleaded guilty before the start of the trial – was found guilty. Rebekah Brooks was found not guilty on all counts. These verdicts unwittingly labelled her as one of the stupidest and most hands-off chief executives ever to have run a large media organization:

Lawyers: So let's get this straight. There was widespread phone-hacking at the *News of the World* and you knew nothing about it?
Brooks: Oh no. I was far too busy doing other things.
Lawyers: Like?
Brooks: Oh, you know . . . Shopping.
Lawyers: Weren't you once editor of the *News of the World* and the *Sun*?
Brooks: Gosh! Now you mention it, I do believe I was. But I ran a very different kind of ship . . .
Lawyers: What kind of ship?
Brooks: I just liked everything to be very relaxed. I wasn't at all hands-on. If a journalist told me he had a good story, I would never bother to ask how he had got hold of it or how accurate it was. I'd just say put it on whatever page you feel like. Just let me choose the photos to go with it.
Lawyers: And did you ever wonder why so many cash payments were being paid to certain people?
Brooks: No. Why should I? £10,000 might be a lot of money

to you, but to me it's loose change. It's the sort of amount I regularly carry around in my bag so that I can pay the cleaner and get a pedicure.

Lawyers: And what about your affair with Andy Coulson?

Brooks: What about it?

Lawyers: For a start, you can tell us how long it went on for.

Brooks: I really don't remember.

Lawyers: Six years?

Brooks: Possibly.

Lawyers: Nine years?

Brooks: Who knows? We were so very much in love that time raced by . . .

Lawyers: And during that time you never once discussed any stories that your papers were running or any office gossip?

Brooks: No, no, no. We just recited Victorian love poetry to one another.

Lawyers: Let's get this clear. You were both senior figures in one of the world's most notoriously controlling organizations and you never once talked of work.

Brooks: So many of the stories our papers wrote were unhappy ones. We liked to talk of happy things.

Lawyers: Not guilty.

It also became apparent in the trial that News International was willing to go the extra mile to protect the feelings of Rebekah Brooks's husband, Charlie:

Charlie: Help! Help!

News International: What is it?

Charlie: The police are coming round to raid our house any minute . . .

News International: So what?

Charlie: The thing is . . . I've got a couple of laptops that are chokka with lesbian porno.

News International: That's terrific, Charlie. Good on you. Anything we can use for Page Three?

Charlie: You don't understand, guys. Bex will go mad if she finds out . . .

News International: You're having a laugh, aren't you? Are you sure you haven't got any other stuff on there that might be incriminating? Because obviously we couldn't help you get rid of that, as that would be illegal.

Charlie: How could you even imagine that?

News International: OK, OK, Charlie. Just had to ask. No offence intended. Now seeing as it's you, here's what we will do. We'll put our best undercover operatives on to this. No expense spared. You'll get a phone call from a pizza-delivery man in an hour or so. He'll say, 'Broadsword calling Danny Boy. Broadsword calling Danny Boy.' You reply, 'The chicken's in the pot,' and then nip down to the car park and chuck your laptop in the rubbish bin.

Charlie: And Bex will never find out?

News International: Absolutely not. But seriously, old boy, are you sure you want to chuck away your porn? *Lesbian Vampire Killers* is one of our all-time favourites and you may find it hard to get another copy.

Murdoch had got his wish. When he had flown into Britain after the hacking of Milly Dowler's phone became public knowledge, he had said that Brooks was his first priority. Three years later she had been cleared of all charges. Coulson's conviction was an acceptable level of collateral damage for his organization. Less so for Cameron, who had to explain why he had employed a criminal as the Tory and Number 10 press spokesman.

The prime minister's apology was a little more genuine than Maria Miller's had been, though scarcely less perfunctory. He had asked Coulson if the phone-hacking stories were true and had been assured they weren't. That was good enough for him. A gentleman's word and all that. Every chap deserved a second chance. There was nothing sinister about Coulson not having been vetted properly. It had just seemed easier not to allow him to see any top-secret documents . . . Cameron carried on in this vein for several days, conveniently ignoring the more obvious point that there had been so much information in the public domain heavily implicating Coulson in criminal activities prior to his appointment that he would always be a serious risk to the government's credibility.

Within a week or so, Coulson and Brooks had dropped out of the news stories, but Cameron wasn't off the hook. The doubts about his lack of judgement were a minor problem compared to the enemies he had made along the way. By making the press and the police, rather than the politicians, the focus of the Leveson Inquiry, he had alienated sections of the media who used to be on his side. Whatever else the Leveson Inquiry turned up during the course of its proceedings, one guaranteed outcome was that there would be a call for greater restrictions on press freedoms – something to which most newspapers were vehemently opposed. Cameron had already lost the un-equivocal support of the Murdoch papers merely by having to be seen to keep his distance from them after the scandal broke, and now other papers, including the powerful *Daily Mail*, turned against him – not by supporting Labour, but by criticizing him personally and backing his opponents on the right. No matter that Cameron frequently made a point of defending press freedoms; his card was marked and there would be no more guaranteed easy rides in some sections of the media.

Cameron wasn't the only Leveson casualty. The Metropolitan Police had been none too happy about their portrayal at the inquiry as a force in bed with dodgy journalists, hanging out in health spas and selling information about public figures for cash. So now the Met's gloves came off too. The Conservative chief whip, Andrew Mitchell, had never been a popular figure with the police security officers who worked in government, some of whom found him brusque and high-handed. In pre-Leveson times, a certain level of self-importance and hauteur from politicians was seen as an occupational hazard. Not any more. A police officer accused Mitchell of calling him a 'fucking pleb' and gave his story to the Murdoch-owned *Sun*. Mitchell denied it, but Cameron sacked him anyway. The prime minister wasn't going to take any more risks giving someone a second chance.

Chapter 11

Brothers in Arms

THERE'S ONE PHONE CALL A NEW PRIME MINISTER LOOKS forward to receiving more than most. It's a tradition that world leaders welcome each other to their exclusive club and, much as a prime minister might like a quick chat with Angela Merkel, the biggest prize is the conversation with the president of the United States. Much preparation – at least at the Number 10 end of the phone line – goes into this short exchange of pleasantries, which will help set the tone for all others. If the two leaders hit it off, then Britain feels itself to be a few inches closer to the centre of world power; if they don't, then Britain is edged out further towards the margins.

In the days of empire and world wars, Britain was an undoubted global power. A country that could back up its rhetoric with a show of enforcement. Since the end of the Second World War, Britain's influence has been on the wane. It may be an advanced economy, a member of the G7, but it has lost status. When a British prime minister speaks, the rest of the world no longer necessarily always bothers to listen. Other countries have become more economically and politically dominant – the USA, Russia, China, Germany – and more will eventually overtake us as emerging economies, such as India and Brazil, reach their growth potential.

Britain's decline in influence is a one-way, irreversible process that is almost impossible for a prime minister to sell to the country. Saying that Britain's power was disproportionately large a hundred years ago, and that we are now slipping back to about where our size and wealth indicate we always should have been, doesn't cut it with an electorate brought up to believe in Britain's natural right to Greatness. A prime minister has to convince both himself and the country that he and they can still make a difference in global politics. To help this process, Winston Churchill coined the phrase 'Special Relationship' to describe the historic closeness of Britain's ties with the US – the assumption being that both countries would watch each other's backs and protect each other's interests.

The Special Relationship had less resonance for America and its presidents. For 'special' they read 'unequal', with the US very much the senior partner. Presidents occasionally paid lip-service to the concept, either when it suited them or as an act of diplomatic goodwill to a junior ally who was visiting their country, but they would never have considered formulating much of their foreign policy around it. Britain, though, had always seen the Special Relationship as something more formal and binding: the basis for Britain as a key player at the table of global geo-politics.

For many years these differences in interpretation were largely cosmetic. Every world leader understood the need for a country to look more important to its own citizens than it actually was – Britain was by no means the only, or worst, offender in this – and successive prime ministers could maintain the illusion of global significance. All worked well, so long as everyone understood the rules of engagement: that the Special Relationship was more of an idealized frame of diplomatic reference than a meaningful or binding arrangement.

It was Tony Blair who unwittingly forced the uneasy pretence at the heart of the Special Relationship into the open. Early on in his time at Number 10, Blair ordered British military interventions in Sierra Leone and Kosovo, both of which were unusually successful and drew plaudits from the international community. Encouraged by this, Blair began to see himself as a global troubleshooter, the wunderkind politician who could march into any conflict zone and bring peace. In Iraq he met his match.

After the 9/11 attacks on the US in 2001, Blair promised the American president, George W. Bush, that he would give him whatever support he needed in the 'war on terror'. The Special Relationship between the two countries demanded that Britain stand 'shoulder to shoulder' with its ally. There was a certain nobility to this sentiment, but it forced Blair into direct conflict with many in his own party and with millions more in the UK. It was clear from the start that the US intended to go to war with Iraq, both as some kind of retribution for 9/11 – even though al-Qaeda hadn't even been operational inside Iraq – and to settle unfinished business from the First Gulf War of 1990–91, but the United Nations was reluctant to sanction a war without just cause and due legal process.

Blair told the British people that the Iraqis had weapons of mass destruction; on that basis Britain went to war. After the invasion, it soon became evident that the Iraqis had no weapons of mass destruction, and many concluded that Blair had exaggerated the Iraqis' military capabilities merely as a pretext for war. He had given his word to the Americans that he would uphold the Special Relationship even to the point of armed conflict, and when the Americans made it known that they were going to invade Iraq regardless of the evidence, he made the decision to go along with them.

In 2014, the Chilcot Inquiry would dither about revealing the private email correspondence between George W. Bush and Tony Blair in the months leading up to the war: not to protect Blair, but to protect the Americans, who, it was felt, might never trust the Brits again were we to make them public. Here was the true one-way-street nature of the Special Relationship. Would the Americans have thought twice about revealing the emails of a British prime minister if their own public was demanding they do so? Doubtful.

The US and UK military invasion of Iraq and presence in Afghanistan all but did for the Special Relationship. Politicians may still have paid lip-service to it when it suited them, but public credibility had been eroded. Although Saddam Hussein was toppled early on in the conflict, there were no quick or easy resolutions. Both the Iraqis and the Afghans were resistant to foreign powers occupying their countries and trying to impose a regime – democratic or otherwise – that would be friendly to the West; and as the fighting stretched into years, and the body bags of soldiers killed in action continued to be flown home almost on a weekly basis with no discernible gain for either side, even those members of the public who had initially supported the war began to question its validity.

What the Iraq War started, the financial crisis completed. The war had been barely affordable – especially for the UK – when the global economy was healthy; when it began to unravel in 2008, politicians and the public in both the US and the UK began to question the cost. When ordinary people were having their standard of living reduced and state benefits and services were being cut at home, a war taking place thousands of miles away with no obvious gains attached began to seem a far less sensible or enticing option for either the US or British government. There was also less personal attachment to prolonging the war, as the two principals, George W. Bush and Tony Blair, had been replaced by Barack Obama and Gordon Brown, but there was still the question of national pride to be considered. Countries don't like to be seen to withdraw from wars because they are running out of cash or are losing: the narrative demands a triumphant success.

Even if the Special Relationship had been fully intact, claiming victory would have been a tough call. With the two countries squabbling over who was most to blame for the recession, it became nearly impossible – especially after a press conference at 10 Downing Street in 2009, the main purpose of which had been to show that Obama and Brown still stood shoulder to shoulder on all the big issues. It went exactly like this:

Nick Robinson, the BBC's political editor: A question for you both, if I may. The prime minister has repeatedly blamed the United States of America for causing this crisis. France and Germany both blame Britain and America for causing this crisis. Who is right? And isn't the debate about that at the heart of the debate about what to do now?
[*With an eye for a tricky question, Brown swivels to hand the hospital pass to Obama. There is a four-second delay before Obama starts speaking.*]

Obama: I, I, would say that, er . . . *pause* . . . if you look at . . . *pause* . . . the, the sources of this crisis . . . *pause* . . . the United States certainly has some accounting to do with respect to . . . *pause* . . . a regulatory system that was inadequate to the massive changes that have taken place in the global financial system . . . *pause, close eyes.* I think what is also true is that . . . *pause* . . . here in Great Britain . . . *pause* . . . here in continental Europe . . . *pause* . . . around the world, we were seeing the same mismatch between the regulatory regimes that were in place and er . . . *pause* . . . the highly integrated, er, global capital markets that have emerged . . . *pause.* So at this point, I'm less interested in . . . *pause* . . . identifying blame than fixing the problem. I think we've taken some very aggressive steps in the United States to do so, not just responding to the immediate crisis, ensuring banks are adequately capitalized, er, dealing with the enormous, er . . . *pause* . . . drop-off in demand and contraction that has taken place. More importantly, for the long term, making sure that we've got a set of, er, er, regulations that are up to the task, er, and that includes, er, a number that will be discussed at this summit. I think there's a lot of convergence between all the parties involved about the need, for example, to focus not on the legal form that a particular financial product takes or the institution it emerges from, but rather what's the risk involved, what's the function of this product and how do we regulate that adequately, much more effective coordination, er, between countries so we can, er, anticipate the risks that are involved there. Dealing with the, er, problem of derivatives markets, making sure we have set up systems, er, that can reduce some of the risks there. So, I actually think . . . *pause* . . . there's enormous consensus that has emerged in terms of what we need to do now and, er . . . *pause* . . . I'm a great believer in looking forwards rather than looking backwards.

It's stretching it to call that press conference a game-changer, but relations between Obama and the British have always been more reserved since then. Obama had come to power in 2008 as the first black president, a man to heal divisions within American society, a man with a reputation as a great public speaker. On his first visit to the UK, he had been made to sound bumbling and incoherent in front of the international media. These things don't get forgotten, even if on the surface nothing appeared to have changed.

Obama was still the first world leader to congratulate Cameron on becoming prime minister, the Special Relationship was still mentioned in their phone call and an invitation to visit the White House was extended. But this was more protocol than genuine warmth. Within a year, when the French president visited America, Obama was declaring, 'We don't have a stronger friend and stronger ally than Nicolas Sarkozy and the French people.' This was a hell of a turnaround from 2003, when the Americans branded the French as 'cowards' and 'traitors' for refusing to join the US and UK in the Iraq War.

This slap to Britain's status – the first of many over subsequent years – didn't stop Cameron from trying publicly to maintain the façade of the Special Relationship. Every prime minister wants to be seen to be close to the power nexus, and Cameron took to posting selfies on his Twitter account of him talking on the phone to Obama. You couldn't imagine the US president taking photos on his mobile of himself talking to Cameron. The prime minister's selfie was ruthlessly parodied on Twitter, but he was undeterred. Even an ersatz proximity was better than none. In July 2014, on his own trip to the US, the Labour leader tried to conjure a photo opportunity of himself meeting Obama as a symbol of his global significance. The Americans offered him something they called a 'brush-by' – a sort of fifteen-minute informal chat around a table. Miliband accepted gratefully.

In private, Cameron and the Coalition recognized that the Special Relationship had minimal residual practical meaning by the time they came to power and, though Gordon Brown had announced the withdrawal of British forces from Iraq at the end of 2008, with the final troops leaving in 2011, there was still the question of what to do about Afghanistan.

In time-honoured fashion, Britain had withdrawn from Iraq claiming nothing less than total victory and the creation of a new Western-style democracy. Life looked rather different on the ground. The Sunni and Shia Muslim sects still battled for control; the country was still rife with outbreaks of violence, and peaceful stability felt a long way off. A more truthful reality was that Gordon Brown had understood that the British people were by and large fed up with the war and had decided to cut his losses.

Cameron was keen to do much the same thing in Afghanistan. He didn't have any personal political investment in maintaining the conflict and was keen to save on military costs. One of the first acts of the Coalition government had been to institute a review of defence spending that would reduce the numbers of regular soldiers in the UK armed services from 102,000 to 80,000 over an eight-year period; ending Britain's commitment to maintaining a substantial military presence in overseas campaigns was integral to making that plan workable. The trick was to leave Afghanistan in a way that looked measured and statesman-like, rather than merely expedient.

The first troop withdrawals were announced in 2011, with Cameron promising that the British numbers in Afghanistan would be reduced from 9,500 to 9,000. A further reduction to 5,000 was scheduled for 2013, with the final troops coming home by the end of 2014. Just in time for the election:

Cameron: Our mission is accomplished.

The army: Really?

Cameron: Just look around you. Happy faces everywhere. I've even brought Michael Owen along to cheer you up.

Michael Owen: Hello, everyone. Fancy a kick-about?

The army: Not much. It's a bit hot and we have to go out on patrol. The Taliban are particularly active at the moment.

Cameron: What's that noise? Is someone having a fireworks party?

The army: No. It's another IED going off.

Cameron: I must say, you chaps have done a brilliant job here. Afghanistan will soon be back to normal. Tourists will soon be flocking here.

The army: You do know that no occupying army has ever won a war in Afghanistan, don't you?

Cameron: There's always a first time. And you men have done wonderfully well to train the Afghan soldiers to take over from you.

Afghan soldiers: To be honest, our hearts aren't in it. We only do it for the money, as we get more from you than we would doing anything else. As soon as you've gone the Taliban will be back in charge.

Cameron: Don't be so silly. Just look at those fields of flowers. Aren't they simply beautiful?

The army: That's the opium crop, Prime Minister. Production is back to pre-war levels.

With the Special Relationship downgraded and a premium being placed on keeping defence costs to a minimum, Britain's foreign policy under the Coalition was forced to walk a tightrope between principled high-mindedness and hard-nosed pragmatism. The decision to commit British troops to overseas military interventions would from now on be based on whether or not it was deemed to be winnable in the short term. The campaign to remove the Libyan leader, Muammar Gaddafi, was very much seen as winnable. In 2004, Tony Blair had decided rapprochement with the dictator was the best way forward; seven years later, with the democratic movements of the Arab Spring gathering strength in North Africa, Nato forces – of which Britain was an integral part – sensed an opportunity to reclaim the moral high ground and remove Gaddafi. The campaign was swift and decisive. 'Gaddafi has left the country and is en route to Venezuela,' said the foreign secretary, William Hague, in February 2011. Gaddafi turned out to be still in an underground bunker in Libya, but in all other respects the Coalition was completely right and Cameron got his moment on the world stage as a defender of the free world. Too bad that Libya has remained in chaos ever since.

Other parts of the globe were more problematic. In 2011 President Assad of Syria, who had previously been looked on by Western leaders as one of the goodish guys, turned out to be brutally repressive in cracking down on peaceful protests aimed at turning his country into a democracy. Within six months the country was locked in a bloody civil war, with Assad allegedly using chemical weapons on his own people. The moral, humanitarian case for Nato and British intervention was just as strong as it had been in Libya. At one point the US seemed keen to intervene, but discretion ruled in the UK; now the Americans were learning that the Special Relationship wasn't necessarily all that special to the Brits when the chips were down. The poodle that had slavishly followed George Bush into Iraq had learned to bark. Or, if not bark, at least growl a bit. This was a war that could be prolonged and messy with few clear good guys or possible winners.

The biggest reality check came in 2014 when Russian troops invaded Ukraine and occupied the Crimea. It was a clear breach of Ukrainian sovereignty that provoked condemnation around the world. William Hague made the extent of his outrage known in a statement to the House of Commons:

Hague: I deplore Russia's actions and have told President Putin in no uncertain terms that he will face severe sanctions from the UK if he does not back down immediately.
Labour: What are these sanctions?
Hague: These sanctions will be in three parts. The first is a visa ban to prevent Russian oligarchs from shopping in Bond Street on Saturdays.
Labour: And the second?
Hague: If the Russians continue to be naughty, we will extend the visa ban to Harvey Nicks.

Labour: The third?
Hague: I'm not going to tell you. Because if I do, the Russians will march straight up to the line in the sand . . .
Labour: And?
Hague: Trample right through it.

Hague uttered these words – or something similar – with as much gravitas as he could muster, but he looked tired and fed up as he said them. He knew he was going through the motions. No one went to war with the Russians any more. Just as no one would go to war with the Americans or the Chinese. To all intents and purposes, these three superpowers were untouchable. They could carve up the world between them. The Middle East was another no-go area; the situations in Syria, Israel, Palestine, Iraq, Iran, Afghanistan and Pakistan were way above Britain's pay grade to resolve. Time was when a British foreign secretary had been a man of substance, a man of global influence. Now he was little more than a diplomatic PR man, trying to lend a few words of comfort and advice here and there while maintaining a British presence on the global stage. A presence that was becoming ever more peripheral. Foreign policy could no longer win a government an election, but it could still lose one. Cameron, whose earlier career had been built in PR, understood all this and didn't mind. Hague, who was more of an old-school politician, did mind. Forty-eight hours after he resigned as foreign secretary in the reshuffle of July 2014, Hague returned to the Commons as leader of the House. He looked happier and more relaxed than he had in years. Who needed the hassle of dealing with America when he had a new Special Relationship with Brangelina to cultivate?

Chapter 12

Bye Bye Blackbird

AFTER THE COALITION CAME TO POWER THERE WERE ALMOST AS many potential threats to Britain's security inside its borders as there were outside. These proved just as difficult to contain: the UK's loss of global influence had even been noted by its own wildlife, which was now threatening to run amok over the whole of the countryside. Something needed to be done.

Over the course of the previous twenty years, the Conservatives had laid themselves open to the same charge that had been levelled at Tony Blair's New Labour: that they were dominated by a metropolitan and Home Counties elite – epitomized by David Cameron and George Osborne – who no longer truly represented the country as a whole. The landowners, farmers, rural working class and the more elderly middle class who had always made up the backbone of Conservative support had begun to feel as if they were being taken for granted.

As fewer and fewer people were living and making their livings in the countryside, the electoral battlegrounds switched to the cities and the suburbs. This is where an election could be won or lost, and policies and resources were concentrated on winning over voters in these areas. A few rural constituencies, especially in the West Country, had fallen to the Lib Dems over the past thirty years, but the Tories reckoned that most of them would continue to return Conservative MPs regardless – through inertia if nothing else – so policy was now seldom targeted specifically at the Tories' traditional support.

In the first half of the twentieth century, the minister for agriculture had been one of the more eye-catching Cabinet posts as farming played a key role in the economy: it was not quite on a par with chancellor, home secretary and foreign secretary, but not far behind. Now, as farming had declined in importance, with more and more food being imported, it was one of the lesser offices of state, rounded up into the catch-all Department for the Environment, Food and Rural Affairs (Defra). Yet not something to be ignored entirely.

Even though many Tory MPs now saw the countryside either as something to be driven through en route to somewhere else or as a summer-holiday destination, they still had an old-fashioned patrician regard for it. The countryside had always been a place to be tamed and controlled – to be knocked into chocolate-box shape – and all the more so now the rest of the world was so resistant to being bossed about by the Brits. The instinct for colonial supremacy had only one remaining outlet: the nation's wildlife. It was their turn to get it in the neck. Better still, they didn't even have a vote.

The first Defra secretary of state for the Coalition was Caroline Spelman. She lasted two years. The primary cause of her downfall was an embarrassing U-turn over a proposal to sell off the UK's forests; she only discovered that almost everyone in the country was opposed to her plan when it was too late to save face. She also made the mistake of misreading the small wind turbine that David Cameron had stuck on the roof of his Notting Hill home while leader of the opposition: its presence had been almost entirely cosmetic, designed more to show that the new Tories had a green heart and cared about environmental issues than to generate any power. It was not to be seen as a sign that the Conservatives were serious about environmental concerns.

Had the Tories not been forced into a Coalition with the Lib Dems, Cameron might have been a little more enthusiastic about alternative energy in government. But green issues were viewed very much as a Lib Dem policy area and, since many on the Tory right had their antennae fine-tuned for any signs that their party might be moving to the left, the new, unspoken brief of Spelman's department was that wind farms and other sources of green energy should be treated with rather more scepticism than they otherwise might. Cameron would become more open about his opposition to onshore wind farms later in his time in office, but in the early days this brief to appease the traditionalists and climate-change sceptics was something to be understood rather than spelled out. Spelman gave the impression that she hadn't even understood it, declaring that 'this government is going to be the greenest ever'. After that, she was bound to struggle.

Spelman was on message in one policy area, though: a badger cull to eliminate TB in cows, something the farming lobby was keen to implement. Her successor, Owen Paterson – a country man on the right of the party, a climate-change sceptic and believer in cutting red tape – was the ideal man both to reassure rural Tories that their values were safe and to push forward the badger cull. To get across the message that he understood all the issues involved, Paterson frequently told reporters he had kept two orphaned badgers, Baz and Bessie, as pets when he was a kid, as if that somehow gave him a hotline into the badger mindset. Maybe it did:

Baz: Stop coughing.
Bessie: Why?
Baz: Because I can hear Owen coming and he doesn't like it.
Owen: Did I hear you coughing?
Baz: It wasn't me . . .
Owen: Open wide, Bessie.
Bessie: Please, please don't kill me, Owen. I promise not to go anywhere near the cows. Besides, it's probably not even TB. More likely it's just bronchitis.
Owen: I'm sorry, Bessie. You know how much I love you, and this is going to hurt me much, much more than it will hurt you.
Bessie: I'm not so sure about that . . .
Owen: Look, just stop whining, will you, and stay where you are while I fetch my rifle.
Baz: It's been nice knowing you, Bessie. I'll just be off now.
Owen: Where do you think you are going, sonny?

Despite many leading animal scientists opposing the cull, arguing it was a mindless and inefficient method of reducing the incidence of TB in cattle, Paterson remained resolute and committed the government to eliminating 30 per cent of the badger population. The cull began in 2013 with two pilot schemes in Gloucestershire and Somerset, where 70 per cent of the badgers were to be shot over a six-week period.

In the event, the cull wasn't quite the bad break for badgers that many environmentalists had feared, as the marksmen who had been employed to shoot them struggled to find their targets. Wisely, many badgers chose to make themselves scarce; in the Gloucestershire zone 35–48 per cent of the badger population was killed; in Somerset that figure was just 27–39 per cent. The costs of the police operation to keep protesters away from the marksmen came to just over £3 million. Or £1,623 per dead badger. Baz and Bessie must have been rolling in their graves at missing out on the chance of becoming, briefly, the most expensive wild animals in Britain.

Despite the failure of the pilot cull, Paterson was determined to roll out the scheme to other areas of the country where bovine TB was particularly prevalent. The blame for the pilot scheme not working was not his but the badgers'. 'They have moved the goalposts,' he declared. How so? By not standing still and making themselves more obvious targets. In 2014, Paterson was forced to abandon his plans to extend the cull after an independent report concluded the scheme had been ineffective and inhumane. Moving the goalposts had paid off: 1–0 to the badgers, even if in Defra's own parallel universe the result was more of a goalless draw; at the department's end-of-year awards ceremony in 2013, the prize for Defra's 'team of the year' went to . . . the badger-control team.

Even before the badgers had come into its sights, the government had already waged war on buzzards. In 2012 Defra proposed a scheme to capture the birds and destroy their nests in order to stop them from killing pheasants that were being reared to be shot. Within a week the buzzards too had moved the goalposts and the plans were shelved: 1–0 to the buzzards. Also in line were cormorants, for making anglers' lives more difficult, along with a lift on the fox-hunting ban that had been introduced by Labour in 2004. Poor old foxes, they didn't know if they were coming or going. One moment they were being chased by dogs, the next they were free to rummage through everyone's garbage to their hearts' content. Now it seemed they might be heading for death row again.

Or perhaps not, as all the government culls seemed to result in victory for the animals concerned. Yet still no species had any guaranteed immunity from the threat of the Paterson chop. Beavers? Starlings? Bats? Newts? Why not? Even robins. They come over here and take over our Christmas cards . . . One Defra insider laughed that if Paterson was given enough time he would work his way through the entire animal alphabet. Unable to impose its will on the rest of the world, the government was forced to exercise its desire for power and control by turning to the natural world. Defra became the filter for the government's pent-up aggression and bloodlust.

Despite this, the only truly successful cull to take place on Defra's watch was that of its minister. In July 2014, Paterson was sacked by Cameron as secretary of state and replaced by Liz Truss, a junior education minister with little previous overt interest in the countryside, in a move primarily designed to increase the number of women on the front benches. Paterson put up a fight worthy of a badger, telling the prime minister that getting rid of him was a 'smash in the teeth for rural voters', that he had done his best to reverse twenty-five years of political correctness and that he was one of the few MPs who stood for traditional Tory values. Cameron was unmoved. In the run-up to the election his need for a media-friendly woman who wouldn't rock the boat was greater than his need for someone who was loud and divided opinion. However fragile the Coalition's influence over the nation's fauna might have been, when it came to a reshuffle the prime minister could still be relied on to get his man – or woman – every time.

Chapter 13

Leader of the Pack

A BIOGRAPHY OF DAVID CAMERON, WRITTEN BY FRANCIS ELLIOTT and James Hanning and published in 2012, described the prime minister's fondness for 'chillaxing' by playing computer games and singing karaoke. Cameron's office immediately countered this, saying his mind was entirely focused on the job, but the image was one that stuck. It may not have been entirely fair – though Cameron didn't do himself any favours by later leaving his eight-year-old daughter in a pub – whoops – and being photographed by his sister-in-law snoozing on an unmade four-poster bed with his red ministerial box by his side – but it did seem to fit. Cameron's personal style was more informal and relaxed than that of previous prime ministers – even Tony Blair – and Cabinet insiders did report he had a hands-off approach to government. Though at times he could lose his temper when things went wrong, his attitude was generally to let people get on with their jobs. He didn't like to micro-manage and his attention to detail was sometimes found wanting.

The chillaxed approach could also be read into his ministerial appointments. It is usual for prime ministers to reshuffle their team on a regular basis – to reward those who have done well, to kick out the dead and the dying, and to give the public a sense of renewal and a feeling that the government is on top of all the key issues of the day. Traditionally, most ministers lasted only a couple of years in office before being moved on, but Cameron rather broke the mould with the Coalition. Though a number of ministers – David Laws, Liam Fox and Chris Huhne – had to resign as a result of their own actions, Cameron's only reshuffle in the early years of his government came in 2012, and even that was notable primarily for how few changes were made.

The one major casualty was the health minister, Andrew Lansley. Managing the NHS is always an uphill struggle – it's a thankless task trying to balance an ageing population that is growing in numbers and expects the latest cutting-edge, expensive medical treatments to be on tap with the same population's unwillingness to pay for the pleasure in increased taxation. It's also an area in which every govern-ment feels obliged to make its mark by correcting the inevitable mistakes of the previous one. But Lansley's reforms – some called them privatization via the back door – were controversial, clumsy and attracted widespread criticism from those working in the NHS. In political terms, Lansley's failure was less the reforms themselves than his lack of charisma. He didn't have the strength of personality to sell his policies to the public or to fend off attacks from the opposition; he looked weak, so he had to go.

Even then, Cameron had a surprise up his sleeve. Jeremy Hunt, the culture and media secretary, who had been under the spotlight for his handling of the BSkyB bid and had also been widely tipped for the axe, found himself promoted to Lansley's job. Two men who hadn't covered themselves in glory: one gets sidelined into the largely honorific role of leader of the House, the other gets promotion. Inevitably, there were suspicions that Hunt wasn't just being rewarded for being more telegenic than Lansley: his support for Murdoch had also been noted.

The other major beneficiary of the 2012 reshuffle was Grant Shapps, a junior housing minister who had been promoted to Conservative party chairman and minister without portfolio in the Cabinet Office. Shapps was a world away from the Oxbridge-educated, entitled elite that made up much of Cameron's inner circle. He was a smart operator who didn't mind making enemies. Which was just as well, as that was something that came easily to him. Before entering parliament, Shapps had owned and run various internet companies, including what he claimed was 'the world's largest internet marketing forum', some of which had been blocked by Google for copyright infringement. He had also run phone lines offering advice to entrepreneurs at £200 per hour while in the Shadow Cabinet.

What was odd about all this was that he had done it using the alias of Michael Green; he had even been photographed at a Las Vegas conference wearing a Michael Green name-tag badge. Shapps had never advertised his dual identity or explained why he had adopted it, though one must assume it was discussed when the prime minister called him into his office to offer him the promotion:

Cameron: Congratulations on the new job.
Shapps: Thank you.
Cameron: There's just one thing I've always wanted to ask . . .

Shapps: Fire away.

Cameron: Why do you have two different names?

Shapps: It's just a bit of rock 'n' roll fun.

Cameron: Sorry?

Shapps: You know how Sting is really Gordon Sumner, Bono is Paul Hewson and Elton John is Reg Dwight? Well, I'm also Michael Green. It's just a stage name.

Cameron: It's not very Westminster. Politics isn't light entertainment.

Shapps: Sure it is. George Osborne changed his name from Gideon . . . And your name isn't really David Cameron, is it?

Cameron: Of course it is. I'm one of the original Berkshire Camerons.

Shapps: No kidding! I always thought it was made up. You live and learn.

What Shapps's appointment said was that dual identity was now something that could be accommodated fairly easily into an MP's CV. A lifestyle choice of a thoroughly modern, multitasking politician that might cause some minor embarrassment when the existence of the doppelgänger was discovered but could be shrugged off and forgotten within a week. More than that, Shapps's appointment showed that Cameron was a tougher, more pragmatic leader than many gave him credit for; a prime minister who understood realpolitik and was willing to work with people whom he did not find naturally simpatico if he saw an advantage in it. Shapps was a shrewd operator who could keep the Tory party in line; a man to whom Cameron could delegate his ruthlessness and thereby keep his own partially hidden a little longer. By 2014, however, it was fully in the open.

Most government operations come pre-briefed, with policy and strategy being leaked to media outlets in advance. It's a way of keeping everyone happy and in the loop; newspapers and TV get the stories they need and the government, by and large, gets to stage-manage their presentation. Criticism can be headed off, the positives can be accentuated and, if things get really bad, then there is still time to change policy on the hoof ahead of its official announcement. Sometimes, though, the government catches everyone – even its own side – by surprise.

The 2014 reshuffle that took place just before the summer recess in July was trailed as being largely cosmetic, a chance to get rid of a few pieces of dead wood and promote some women. Despite having frequently spoken out on gender equality, Cameron had few women on his front benches. This had left him open to accusations that either he didn't practise what he preached or that he thought there were no talented women in the Tory party, both of which the opposition had exploited relentlessly. Promoting women, then, was assumed to be the prime purpose of any reshuffle.

With less than a year left in office before the election, there wouldn't be time for any new minister to effect any real change in their department. In fact, even if they wanted to, in some departments the brief was to do as little as possible. For example, as secretary of state for transport, Patrick McLoughlin's trickiest jobs were to keep the two most contentious issues – the siting of a new London airport and the high-speed rail link from London to Birmingham (and beyond) – at arm's length until after the election. The directive from Number 10 to all departments was to not rock the boat by doing something that might alarm the electorate; just sit back and let the prime minister and the chancellor concentrate on the economic recovery. For the most part, government was to be image-management rather than executive action.

The initial signs were that the reshuffle would be as predicted. Old-timers, such as Europhile Ken Clarke, who had served his purpose in preserving continuity and was a liability now that Cameron wanted to prevent Tory voters migrating to Ukip, were gently moved along. In came a powerful group of women who could be relied on to stay on the party message. Then came the bombshells. Cameron's four most senior ministers – chancellor, foreign secretary, home secretary and education secretary – had all been in post since the Coalition had come to office, a rare occurrence in any government, and it had been assumed they would remain there for the final year. Not so.

The departure of William Hague as foreign secretary was the first surprise, though he had looked an increasingly isolated figure on the front bench. When a foreign secretary appears far more comfortable being photographed next to Angelina Jolie and Brad Pitt at a conference on ending war rape than he does with his colleagues, it's probably time to move on. The bigger shock was Michael Gove's departure from the Department of Education:

Cameron: Ah, Michael. Good of you to come . . .
Gove: I wasn't aware I had a choice.
Cameron: I've got some great news for you. As you know, I think you've been doing a brilliant job. You've transformed education. So now I'm going to promote you . . .

Gove: Thank you very much.

Cameron: . . . to chief whip.

Gove: I see . . . Help me out a little here. In what sense exactly is this a promotion? Chief whip is just an enforcing apparatchik.

Cameron: In the sense that you're actually just too good to be at education. Or anywhere else. Your real talents lie more behind the scenes. A long way behind the scenes.

Gove: So . . . it is a genuine promotion, then?

Cameron: Of course. Have a read of the press release: 'Michael Gove is being promoted to chief whip.' It's there in black and white, so it must be true.

Gove sounded less than convinced later that day when talking to the BBC. 'Demotion, emotion, locomotion, promotion: I don't know how you would describe this move,' he said. No one else was in much doubt. Gove had paid the price for the twin crimes of toxicity and ambition. As secretary of state for education, he had been the most dynamic and ideological of all the Coalition's ministers; within weeks of getting his foot in the door he had initiated his programme to reform England's schools with the introduction of parent-led free schools and a return to what he saw as an 'old-fashioned education system, underpinned with traditional British values'. It was an approach that played well with a Middle England that had become anxious about a fall in educational standards that it linked to a rise in politically correct multiculturalism; but it was also one that had put him on a collision course with most teachers and headteachers, who had been extremely vocal in their opposition.

Relations between the two sides had become so poor that even when Gove had a good idea it was shouted down and got the government bad headlines. Even though he was one of the most accomplished performers in the House of Commons, regularly swatting aside his Labour opposite number – the wet-behind-the-ears Tristram Hunt, who had been promoted rather too quickly and whose own policies seemed to change by the week – Gove had an image problem with the public.

Like so many things in politics, it wasn't entirely fair. There were other ministers much more deserving of the chop. Iain Duncan Smith, secretary of state for work and pensions, had been responsible for one of the most disastrous roll-outs of any government policy: the universal credit, a welfare reform designed to replace six means-tested benefits and tax credits. After three years, the government watchdog the Major Projects Authority had declared the universal credit programme to be such an abject failure that it must now be deemed an entirely different project from the one originally proposed. The only person unaware of just how disastrous his flagship benefits reforms had been was IDS himself. In one session of ministerial questions his shadow minister, Rachel Reeves, pointed out, 'There are now 5,610 people enrolled on universal credit. At the current rate of progress, it will be another 1,052 years before he reaches his target of 7.8 million.' Duncan Smith was outraged at this slur. 'Universal credit is entirely on schedule,' he insisted. How did he know? Because he had just changed the timetable. IDS is the sort of person who could argue that the reason terminally ill patients have not received their sickness benefits is because they have had the cheek to live longer than expected.

Labour knew that Duncan Smith was a walking disaster area as work and pensions secretary. The Tories and the Lib Dems knew it too. The only people who didn't were the Tory voters. Or if they did, it wasn't going to lose them much sleep. Making life unnecessarily miserable for the un-employed or the long-term sick – collectively known as 'scroungers' – was not their major concern. So IDS got to survive as minister through a combination of, first, Cameron not wanting to hand over the poisoned chalice of sorting out the universal credit system to an up-and-coming politician whose career might suffer from the experience and, second, there being no pressure on the prime minister to alter the status quo.

Had it just been a matter of toxicity, Gove might have survived, as he was a popular and effective politician within government, if not without. What did for him was his vanity and ambition. It's what does for many politicians in the end. While some MPs are happy to remain backbenchers, serving their constituencies loyally and hoping to be rewarded with a junior, backwater ministerial post one day – Labour's Chris Mullin, whose parliamentary diaries of a nobody are works of measured, moral, comic understatement, comes to mind – there are many other, more alpha, personalities for whom Westminster is a path to advancement. Politicians for whom loyalty isn't just a matter of principle but a commodity to be traded for preferment. Gove was one such man.

Keeping all his ministers happy is often a trickier bal-ancing act for a prime minister than running the country. Especially when the job some of them really want is his. Although for Cameron becoming prime minister might have been the fulfilment of some childhood destiny, for other politicians the realization of the possibility is more slow-burning. Gove had been a journalist on *The Times* before entering parliament, and education had always been the main focus of his political campaigning; he had been Cameron's natural and obvious choice to become education minister. But in his four years at the Department of Education his potential to go further had been noticed; as early as 2012 the former Tory politician Michael Portillo had marked him out as a possible future leader of the Conservative party.

Such attention can't fail to turn a politician's head, even if she or he had never previously harboured any serious ambitions in that area. It is a conferment of status, an assumed power. Gove had never said he wanted to be party leader, but he hadn't needed to, as the great thing about political life is that any statement of future ambition can be interpreted in any number of ways.

'I have no intention of standing for party leader' could mean:

1. I have no intention of standing for party leader.
2. I have no intention of standing for party leader at this time, though this could change tomorrow.
3. I have every intention of standing for party leader this very minute.

Similarly, his saying, as he once did, 'I am backing George Osborne for party leader' could mean:

1. I am backing George Osborne for party leader.

2. I am backing Boris Johnson for party leader.
3. I am backing myself for party leader.

Whether he really did want to be the next party leader, preferred to position himself as kingmaker, thought his best chance was to wait and let someone else take over from Cameron before making his move, or genuinely was happy to remain where he was were all equal possibilities. The only thing that was certain was that he didn't want anyone pushing themselves above him in the queue for the job. The official pecking order was George Osborne, Boris Johnson and then Michael Gove. So when the home secretary, Theresa May, looked as though she might be nudging her way ahead of him, something needed to be done. It was the undoing of them both.

The spat between the education secretary and the home secretary started when Gove told *Times* journalists over dinner in June 2014 that the Home Office hadn't done enough to prevent Islamic radicals from infiltrating schools in Birmingham. May responded by posting an inter-departmental letter on the Home Office website saying that Gove had ignored the problem for years. Though the issue was ostensibly about extremism, the subtext was a power struggle between the two ministers. Both had been ear-marked as possible future party leaders; neither was willing to back down.

At a time when the prime minister wanted to put on a show of party unity – to convince the country that the Conservative hierarchy was a happy, collegiate team – the row came as both a distraction and an embarrassment. Cameron immediately put Gove and May on the naughty step: they were both forced to come to the Commons to answer urgent questions. They looked like sheepish school-children as they sat on the front bench with the government's bouncer-in-chief, Eric Pickles, sitting between them to make sure there was no more fighting. First in line was May.

'The education secretary has apologized,' she declared. At which point Gove winced. That didn't seem to be the way he remembered it. When his turn came, he did his best to look and sound contrite, but couldn't quite manage it. Like May, he is a politician who has never knowingly been wrong about anything.

Gove and May left the chamber that afternoon both for-given and unforgiven. On the surface, Cameron had made his point. Prime ministers are always wise to consider the temporal nature of their position, but most prefer to do so in abstract terms: a death that will happen at some unspecified, far-off date in the future. They do not want their minds concentrated: and when they are, they want it to be on their own terms; they want the succession to be something in their gift, a baton to be handed on to a person – and at a time – of their own choosing. Gove's and May's public contretemps had been an unwelcome reminder that a prime minister frequently doesn't get his own way in these matters and that the vultures would be circling for Cameron if he couldn't win an overall majority in May 2015. His revenge was Gove's demotion to chief whip. May remained in post, though not unscathed. She had been in line for a possible move to the Foreign Office; being made to stay at the Home Office – where she had both to explain the delays in the pass-port office that in summer 2014 led to some people missing their foreign holidays ('More people than expected wanting to renew their passports and go abroad is a sign the government's long-term economic plan is working' didn't quite cut it as an excuse) and to account for the disappearance of 114 files relating to a possible cover-up of paedophile activities by politicians and other public figures in the 1980s – was her punishment. Cameron might have been keen to have more women in prominent roles, but only some women. The right women, who could be relied on to see no evil, hear no evil and speak no evil.

Behind Cameron's new ruthlessness, some detected the hand of Lynton Crosby – the Australian 'master of the dark political arts' who had been brought in to run the Conservative election campaign. Others reckoned the prime minister was simply revealing his true colours: Cameron was now just as at home culling his friends as culling his enemies. The prime minister and Andrew Lansley, the leader of the House, had been close since before Cameron entered parliament and, even though Lansley had been removed as health minister in 2012, there had always been an understanding that he would be looked after. In the 2014 reshuffle, Lansley was expecting to be moved on to Brussels as European commissioner. Cameron couldn't oblige, as the job had become more politically complicated than anticipated, and he nominated Lord Hill, the former leader of the Lords, instead. The customary resignation letters exchanged between Lansley and the prime minister, after the former was reshuffled out of a job, were telling:

Lansley: 'Earlier this year, I told you that I did not intend to stand again at the next election. You supported my ambition to continue my life of public service in challenging and

185

important roles. I am grateful to you now for expressing your support for me to take such a role in international public service in the months ahead.'

Cameron: 'I would like you to know how much I have appreciated your friendship, loyalty and support over the years. You have much more to give in terms of public service, and I look forward to being able to support you in doing so in the months and years ahead.'

As a dismissal, it couldn't have been more telling or more crushing. Cameron had offered Lansley nothing more than a casual brush-off; a vague promise of helping out in some minor way at some unspecified point in a distant future. All friendships were now on hold. What mattered was winning the election, and winning the election meant presenting the right party image at all times.

Chapter 14

I Believe I Can Fly

A DEGREE IN POLITICS, PHILOSOPHY AND ECONOMICS (PPE) FROM Oxford University is often described as a passport to power. Of the current Cabinet, David Cameron, William Hague, Jeremy Hunt, Philip Hammond and Danny Alexander all studied PPE. As did Ed Miliband and Ed Balls on the opposition front benches and thirty other MPs in the Commons. By any standards, it is a remarkably concentrated gene pool; no other degree course at a single university can currently match it for producing high-ranking politicians.

Oxford likes to talk of its PPE success in terms of the quality of its intake and the breadth of its course. Former students joke about how its informal academic structure of just three or four tutorials a week gave them sufficient flexibility to plot their future careers – often starting with the presidency of the Oxford Union. Both viewpoints are true, but miss the bigger picture. The reason so many PPE graduates become politicians is because the course is self-selecting.

No student is going to be admitted on to the course unless he or she has achieved the very best academic results and is extremely self-confident and self-motivated; almost invariably these students will be from white, middle-class backgrounds, will have been to an independent or selective state school, and will have parents and teachers who have encouraged them to aspire to an Oxford education and a high-flying career. Oxford's PPE course has also produced many successful BBC journalists, such as Nick Robinson, Evan Davies and Ian Katz, along with dozens of others working on national newspapers. While some students may come to Oxford with a career plan already in place, more will do so because it offers them a near guarantee of being able to realize whatever they decide to do; their later careers are just a by-product of their potential.

PPE has no powers of indoctrination and no hidden agenda to produce a certain type of graduate. The students make the political, philosophical and economic connections they were always going to make. Those on the right have their right-wing views reinforced; those on the left have their left-wing views reinforced. All that happens in the three years in between is that everyone becomes a bit better informed and a lot more confident that they are right. And that they are the right people for any job they want – a view that is in turn reinforced because many of the applicants they are up against are also PPE graduates. The social connections that are forged at Oxford make them masters of the universe: satellites of power that continue to orbit one another throughout their careers.

PPE is a Westminster curiosity, an illuminating window into the mechanics of power. Yet it is also a red herring. Nick Clegg didn't do PPE at Oxford. Nor did hundreds of other MPs. But as far as the general public is concerned, they might as well have done. Any snobbery that may exist about what university an MP may have attended, or what course they studied, is confined almost entirely within the walls of Westminster. When asked by Jeremy Paxman on *Newsnight* if it rankled that Cameron had got a first when he had only got a 2:1, Boris Johnson, whose degree was in classics, said, 'It would if it wasn't that his first was in PPE.' The implication that classics is a harder degree than PPE was a distinction only someone who had been to Oxford would make.

No one else cares. To the rest of the country most of the politicians look pretty much identical: white, male, middle-class and metropolitan. Women, working-class men and those born and living in rural areas are the exception: outliers. For all their insistence on the differences between them, in all the most important areas the three party leaders are nearly identical:

Cameron: I'm not really that posh at all. I can get on with anyone. I even considered going to Africa on my gap year to help make a Kenyan tribe self-sufficient in water.
Miliband: Well, I actually met a few black kids at my North London school, so I am much more in touch with real people than you.
Cameron: Did you invite any home for high tea?
Miliband: Er, no. I didn't know them that well. Besides, we only had Earl Grey and I don't think they would have liked that.
Clegg: I've always been much more of a European myself.
Miliband: Before or after leaving Westminster?
Clegg: I used to hang out in Paris on the Left Bank, smoking Gauloises, listening to Jacques Brel and setting fire to cacti. I've seen life from the wrong side of the tracks.

Miliband: I was always more of an N-Dubz fan, myself. Or so I've been told to say, as they went to the same school as me.

Cameron: You can't beat Coldplay. Saw them at the O2. Sensational.

Miliband: Did either of you see the stage adaptation of *Wolf Hall*?

Cameron: I had tickets for the opening night. Couldn't go, sadly.

Clegg: It was brilliant, wasn't it? Though didn't you find the seats terribly uncomfortable?

Miliband: Awful. My back played up for days afterwards.

Here is the leaders' dilemma. Despite their very obvious similarities, they need to differentiate themselves from one another. The personal has become public. In former times, politicians were judged far more on their actions than on the way they conducted their private lives. No one minded so much if a prime minister regularly drank too much or was having an affair, because such gossip wasn't so widely reported or commented on. Now it is everyone's business, and politicians can't just lay all the blame on an inquisitive media. They themselves have increasingly sought out the media to sell an idealized, personable version of themselves – if they can appear likeable and normal, voters will be more inclined to trust their policies – and there is no going back just because the rules of the game have changed, with newspapers and television becoming more intrusive than their subjects might like.

Aware that their backgrounds were actually quite different from most of those they sought to represent, the image that

Cameron, Miliband and Clegg most frequently sought to portray was the precise opposite of their real selves: the illusion that they were normal, regular guys who were in touch with the everyday concerns of ordinary people. The sort of men you might want to sit down and have a drink with in a pub. By and large, the harder they tried, the more they failed, more often than not giving the impression of behaving like minor celebrities rather than normal men. It wasn't easy for them to be otherwise, with journalists and photographers picking over everything, from hair loss to weight gain. But even so . . . ordinary people usually just get mildly pissed off that they are going bald or getting a bit porky, and then they get on with their lives. Politicians seem to react with panic, adopting hairstyles and diets prescribed by a focus group of image consultants.

Normality is an elusive, moving target. A politician can never appear to be caught on the hop. Saying 'To tell you the truth, I've never heard of it and I don't much care either way' about something isn't an option. They have to care, but in the right sort of way. Taste in music is subject to similar levels of scrutiny. Before appearing on Radio 4's *Desert Island Discs*, each of the party leaders agonized over the eight selections that would present him in the best light. The choices needed to be mainstream and catholic, music that would make him look interesting – though not too interesting, as anything too avant-garde might frighten off the voters – and reflect a broad spectrum of taste: 'I can't stand pop music and only listen to Bach' was another sentence on the proscribed list. If the politician actually liked the music that he chose for *Desert Island Discs*, it was a bonus.

Holidays were taken in locations that would look good to

voters. Nothing too flash was allowed; long-haul flights to five-star resorts in the Maldives were a no-no. A week or two by the coast in Britain always played well, but European destinations such as France, Spain, Portugal, Italy and Greece were more than acceptable. These were the kinds of holidays ordinary people might take; except they weren't, of course, because Cameron et al were renting expensive private villas rather than staying in a resort. Nor were they reading the same kinds of books. Before they left for their holidays, politicians were often asked what books they would be taking with them; their lists always included one classic, a novel that had been tipped to make the Booker shortlist, a political autobiography and a heavyweight economics handbook: in 2014, Thomas Piketty's *Capital in the Twenty-First Century* was a must-read. What was missing was any sign of the latest Jo Nesbo thriller or an admission that they might not finish reading their books because they'd keep nodding off on the sun-lounger.

Then there were the holiday photo opportunities: newspapers always liked to have a snap of the prime minister on vacation and Cameron always obliged by posing with his wife, Sam, in a local fish market. Only again it wasn't the sort of holiday experience most people have, because most normal couples can't spend fifteen minutes in a market together without having a row. Here is the next illusion: that all party leaders must conform to the norm of being happily married to someone of the opposite sex and must appear in public to be the senior partner in the relationship. Though the rules for political husbands differ from those for wives. Denis Thatcher was allowed to be a grumpy, remote – slightly comical – background figure; a man happy to swig a

G&T in the golf club while his wife got on with the job. Wives are expected to be more docile and connected.

Cameron, Miliband and Clegg all married strong, successful women. Samantha Cameron was the creative director of the stationery company Smythson; Justine Thornton, Miliband's wife, was a barrister; Miriam Clegg was a partner in an international law firm. Yet only Sam Cam played the political PR game by appearing in public to defer slightly to her husband. She did it perfectly. With the dolphin tattoo on her ankle suggestive of a more transgressive, independent past, she came across as a twenty-first-century woman with a keen sense of her own self, who believed in sexual equality but was sensible enough to allow her husband to have the final word on the manly issues of what car or lawnmower they should buy and what Britain's position should be on the conflict between Israel and the Palestinians in Gaza. This was the country's preferred state of political marriage.

Miliband and Justine had been a couple for nearly ten years and had two children before they got married in 2011. Although Miliband said it had always been their plan to get married at some point, the timing looked anything but coincidental. It had been OK for a politician to be living with his partner while he was a minister on the way up, but now that he was a party leader with aspirations to run the country, his domestic arrangements needed to be changed to something more conventional. Something that reflected the gravitas of the job. It was as if he feared his capacity for commitment might be doubted unless he was married. As with so many aspects of modern political life, it was a lose–lose situation for Miliband. If he hadn't got married there would have been mutterings from some quarters about the status of his relationship; and when he did get married there were grumbles that it had been done primarily for career purposes.

The appearance of normality is hard-won for any politician. Justine never looked as comfortable as Samantha appearing in public alongside her husband. There was no reason why she should, but it still counted against her and Ed. Somehow they were less than something they were meant to be, no matter how hard they worked at it. Before the 2015 election, Labour announced that Justine was going to take a more prominent role in the campaign than she had done previously, in a bid to scoop up women's votes and make her husband look normal. It was a role she must have been dreading.

Miriam Clegg chose to make the minimum engagement with her husband's public life. She had her career, he had his. She'd turn up to support him when absolutely necessary, but otherwise he was on his own. Nor was she going to be bound by being on her husband's Lib Dem message. If she had something to say, she'd say it; and if she didn't, she'd keep quiet. If people couldn't tell the difference between her own private opinions and the public views of her husband, then it was their problem. This was by far the most liberated, most modern stance of any of the leaders' spouses and it should have counted in Nick's favour, marking him out as a man completely at ease in an equal relationship. Instead, it was a mark against him. The country wasn't entirely ready for its senior politicians to embrace the twenty-first century. There was some grudging respect for him, but the main way Clegg's marriage played out in the media was that he was in some way a hen-pecked husband, who wasn't quite able to keep his wife in line. Rather than being a woman who knew her own mind, Miriam was marked out as a ball-breaker. This image fed conveniently into Clegg's other key relationship:

Miriam: Make the kids their breakfast, will you?
Clegg: I'm a wee bit busy this morning. Can't you?
Miriam: Don't be difficult.
Clegg: OK, darling. You haven't forgotten that we're going to this dinner tonight, have you?
Miriam: Oh shit. I had. I've got a meeting. You'll have to go on your own.
Clegg: Are you sure you can't get out of your meeting?
Miriam: Don't be silly. I'm off now. Make sure the kids get to school on time.
Clegg: Morning, Dave.
Cameron: Not now, Nick. I'm seeing George in an hour and I need time to prepare.
Clegg: Can I help?
Cameron: Just leave me alone for now.
Clegg: How about a spot of lunch at one? I've got a couple of hours free.
Cameron: I'm tied up with the Chinese first minister today. Another time . . .
Clegg: Tomorrow?
Cameron: No.

Despite the self-evident limitations and irritations arising from the conflation of the public and the private in political life, it was hard to feel too much sympathy for any of the political leaders. It wasn't as if they had been under any illusions about what their jobs would entail when they ran for public office; no one had forced them to become leaders, and the decision to take the personal hits that would inevitably ensue must have been made jointly as a family. If they hadn't since been able to work the system to their advantage and it had all been a great deal trickier to manage than they had hoped, then no one could say they hadn't been warned.

Cameron undoubtedly got the easiest ride. Not just because his marriage fitted the expected template better, but because he seemed personally more suited to his position. Though all three wore the mantle of entitlement, Cameron wore it best. He wasn't embarrassed by it; his patrician upbringing gave him the air of someone used to connecting with the lower classes in a 'Hail, good fellow, well met. Would you like a pint of ale?' kind of way. It wasn't ideal, but it did at least have the virtue of sincerity. Cameron might have preferred to look rather more down to earth than he was, but he came across as he was: a posh boy with limited experience of the world who was probably fundamentally a decent bloke when he wasn't being prime minister. If push came to shove and you had to spend an hour or two chatting to him, you could probably rub along reasonably OK.

All this was less true for Clegg, who carried with him the desperation of his own political position, the guilt of his entitlement and the tortured air of someone who wished he could turn back the clock to April 2010. But the one with the biggest image problem was Miliband. Over and above any sense of awkwardness in his role as party leader, he looked so obviously awkward in himself. Those who have spent time with him in private say he is charming, funny and engaged. Everything he is not when out meeting the public; there he looks gauche, clumsy and as if he has never had contact with anyone who isn't a metropolitan, middle-class intellectual.

To begin with, the Labour strategy team's solution to Miliband's image problem was to ignore it; to appear as if they were above such a petty level of engagement. Cameron might have the polish, but Miliband had both the sincerity and the policies. His message was, 'Listen to what I say, not the way I say it.' In an ideal world, this would have been a reasonable response: politics should be about ideas and substance rather than being a beauty parade. But it isn't. Presentation is just as important as the policies themselves – especially when, like Miliband in his first few years, he didn't even have many policies of his own to promote. Voters knew what he was against, but they didn't have much idea what he was for. So presentation was all there was.

Year after year, the opinion polls kept telling the same story. Labour was consistently ahead of the Conservatives as a party, but Miliband was way behind Cameron in the personal ratings. Voters didn't connect with him and didn't see him as prime ministerial material. The harder Miliband tried to make himself look like a normal human, the more nerdy and awkward he became. His lowest point was reached during the European election campaign of May 2014. First he was caught out on ITV's *Good Morning Britain* chat show, when, having campaigned strongly on 'the cost-of-living crisis' under the Tories, he was asked how much his own family spent on their weekly food shop. Miliband looked startled and replied, 'We probably spend £70 or £80 on groceries.' The presenter, Susanna Reid, then told him that an average family of four generally spent over £100. Miliband's face fell along with his personal ratings: he knew he had blown it. Few party leaders have time to push trolleys round a supermarket, but rather than make a joke about how Justine or the au pair did most of the shopping because he couldn't be trusted to get the right things, he panicked. He didn't want to look too sexist about the division of the household chores, nor too privileged. Having no real idea how much his family spent, he wanted to come in on the low side to avoid accusations that he was living it up on prosciutto and prosecco while the rest of the country was making do with scraps. So he offered his best lowest guess, got it wrong, looked out of touch and undermined his cost-of-living campaign.

Worse was to follow the next day when he struggled to eat a bacon sandwich. In his hands, a staple snack for many families became a dangerous, alien object with a life of its own that indiscriminately dripped ketchup and grease. Humiliatingly for Miliband, an aide grabbed the half-eaten sandwich out of his hand and passed it to someone else rather than letting him finish it. He couldn't even be trusted with a bacon sandwich.

Miliband's biggest image problem, though, was the way he spoke. He didn't talk in familiar, everyday English; his speeches sounded as if they had been written and delivered by a computer programmed to write in policy-wonk speak. Some sentences were barely intelligible to his audience; they might even have been barely intelligible to him if he had been made to listen to a recording of them. The lower his ratings fell, the less passion he projected.

Something had to give, and in July 2014 Miliband went on the offensive, deliberately referring to his awkwardness and trying to make a virtue of it: he wasn't a walking photo opportunity, but he could be trusted with the important things. This would have sounded better if he hadn't spent so much of the previous four years trying to turn himself into a photo opportunity.

During his time as party leader, several image consultants, including autism expert Dr Simon Baron-Cohen, had been employed to knock Miliband into shape:

Therapist 1: Today's lesson is spontaneity.
Miliband: Isn't that scheduled for tomorrow?
Therapist 1: Yes. But I thought I'd bring it forward.
Miliband: I'd rather stick with the original plan, if you don't mind.
Therapist 2: OK, then. We will continue with your plain English course. Please translate the following sentence: 'The new agenda is that we need to care about the model of the economy we have and the distribution of income it creates; we need to care about predistribution as well as redistribution.'
Miliband: 'The new agenda is that we need to care about the model of the economy we have and the distribution of income it creates; we need to care about predistribution as well as redistribution.'
Therapist 3: Let's move on to empathy. Try to imagine I'm a man whose wife has just died after waiting more than twelve hours in Accident and Emergency without being treated. What would you say to him?
Miliband: I can assure you that under Labour, A&E waiting times will be reduced to a maximum of three hours.

The natural inference of Miliband's U-turn on his own image problems was that Labour's remedial measures hadn't worked. The party strategists had realized they would have to play the last ten months with one hand tied behind their backs and hope the voters could be persuaded that the old Miliband, whom they had thought was odd, was actually the new-hearted, connected Miliband.

In image terms, it was advantage Cameron, though he was far from home and dry. First he had to make sure that an electorate that had been encouraged by both politicians and the media to focus on surface-image issues did not make the connection that the policies themselves might be equally confected to look good for short-term party-political gain rather than the long-term good of the country. Then he also had to watch his back for trouble from elsewhere.

Chapter 15

Don't Think Twice, It's All Right

THERE'S AN OLD SAYING THAT ALL POLITICAL CAREERS END IN failure. It's not quite true. Some careers end with revenge – something all party leaders need to bear in mind before shuffling ministers out of Cabinet and on to the back benches. In Westminster, out of sight is not always out of mind and some MPs are rather more dangerous to their own side out of office than they are in it, as the basic rules of collective responsibility and party loyalty no longer necessarily apply. Former ministers – or shadow ministers – who have no prospect of further promotion and are not angling for a seat in the House of Lords or a place on a government quango in return for their compliance have little to fear from stepping out of line; as long as they are still popular within their constituencies, their party leaders are stuck with them.

The damage done by a former minister can be devastating. In 1990, Geoffrey Howe resigned as deputy prime minister over Margaret Thatcher's handling of relations with the European Union. Not previously noted for his oratory – the Labour chancellor Denis Healey had once described an attack from him as like 'being savaged by a dead sheep' – Howe delivered a resignation speech in the Commons that proved to be the catalyst for the series of manoeuvrings within the Tory party that brought an end to Thatcher's eleven years in office.

Few outgoing politicians have had such a damaging effect on their leaders as Howe, but then they haven't needed to or wanted to. The threat of doing so is often sufficient. In any case, politicians are not always motivated by settling scores: many just want to make sure their place in history is understood and judged to be as important as they themselves believe it to be. The most straightforward way of doing this is for a politician to write his memoirs or diaries.

This won't necessarily be lucrative. Publishers have been a great deal stingier with their advances since David Blunkett was paid in the region of £400,000 for an autobiography that left out much of the detail of his personal life and sold fewer than 5,000 copies in total, but even a small name with a small story can usually be guaranteed a deal of some sort. For a politician who just wants a platform, this is more than enough.

The big names can still command top dollar and UK politicians didn't come much bigger than Tony Blair in the early years of the twenty-first century. His autobiography came out almost at the same time as Ed Miliband became leader. Miliband, though, had little to fear: he had only entered parliament in 2005 and had barely registered on his former leader's consciousness. Blair was more interested in absolving himself of blame for anything and in running down Gordon Brown. The book's main curiosity was that it was written in the style of an enthusiastic teenager with rather too many exclamation marks:

If only Iraq had been that simple. I know there are some of you out there who want me to apologize, but life isn't that simple when there's a war-crimes indictment at stake. Look, I feel the deaths of our servicemen every bit as keenly as if the bullets had pierced me like stigmata, but sometimes one has to just stand up and do the right thing even if the evidence isn't there. OK, I will admit I did have a bit of a wobbly – Cherie had to give me big cuddles, know what I mean! – when it turned out Saddam didn't have WMD, but I honestly never lied about them. It was just one, small, teeny mistake and everyone tore me to pieces! Give us a break! And for the record I didn't always have a plan to go to war. The first I heard of it was when Statesman George – Top bloke! Top thinker! – phoned to say US troops were going in!

I was pretty fed up when everyone failed to see what we had achieved in Iraq, but an audience with the Pope, who said, 'It is you who should be baptizing me,' soon cheered me up. And I felt a sense of duty to protect the country from Gordon's incompetence. 'You're just waiting until everything's about to go pear-shaped,' he would yell. As if! It was only my darling John Prescott's desire to be out of the limelight as my deputy that prompted my resignation.

Neither did Miliband have much to worry about from other outgoing politicians, who were also more concerned about securing their reputations. And knocking the former leader, Gordon Brown. Alistair Darling, who had been Labour chancellor throughout the financial crisis, published his 'non mea culpa', *Back from the Brink*, in 2011:

The collapse of Northern Rock in September 2007 was the first sign that anything was at all wrong in the British economy. And I must say, though I say so myself, I handled the crisis exceedingly well. I don't want to cast blame on either Mervyn King or Gordon Brown – both of whom I hold in the highest esteem – but their incompetence and intransigence made finding a solution extremely difficult and it was only my brilliance in offering guarantees to all savers that averted financial meltdown.

I have always regarded Gordon with the utmost respect, even though he clearly thought I was a bit of an idiot, and it saddens me to have to say his years as PM were the most disastrous in living memory. It could all so easily have been different had he listened to me. He appeared weak within months of taking office, by dithering over whether to hold a general election. Had he bothered to ask me, I would have advised him not to. There was no point in taking a chance on losing an election when there was the guarantee of doing so in 2010.

Gordon Brown has so far held fire on his own memoirs, though it's not hard to imagine who his targets might be when he gets round to writing them. Three other heavyweights of the Blair–Brown years – Alan Johnson, Peter Hain and Jack Straw, who had chosen to remain in parliament – also used their time out of office to publish their memoirs. Johnson had been Labour's shadow chancellor for the first year of the Coalition, before voluntarily returning to the back benches for personal reasons. His memoir, *This Boy*, was the odd one out. It was well written, focused entirely on his West London childhood and sold well. Hain's *Outside In* was a more traditional offering:

'Ah, Peter, return of the prodigal son!' Nelson Mandela beamed, welcoming me to his Johannesburg home in February 2000. 'Thank God you've come back. All South Africa has been praying for your return.' 'Thank you for taking care of things in my absence,' I replied, handing him my coat. 'And I have something for you, Peter,' he said, with a twinkle. He left the room and came back with a book. 'It's a copy of my latest bestseller.' Tears welled in my eyes when I read the title: *Peter Hain: A Long Walk to Aberystwyth*, by Nelson Mandela.

I make no apologies for supporting the Iraq War. The simple fact is that Tony wanted there to be WMD in the country and I was happy to support him in that. Besides which, it would have been wrong for us to have allowed the US to act against Iraq unilaterally. Bilaterally was so much better. For some reason it became much harder for Labour to retain the country's trust after Iraq, but I did derive much satisfaction from finally bringing peace in our time to Northern Ireland. The negotiations between Gerry Adams and Ian Paisley were often difficult. How glad I was to be able to call on Nelson Mandela. 'Ask yourselves what Peter would do,' he told them both.

Straw's autobiography, *Last Man Standing*, fell somewhere in between Johnson's and Hain's: one part well-written memoir of a difficult childhood to one part self-serving non-apologia. It, too, did Miliband no harm. The Labour leader did take one small hit, though, when Gordon Brown's former special adviser, Damian McBride, timed the publication of his autobiography to coincide with the Labour party conference in 2013. Miliband himself didn't come in for much personal criticism, but the portrait that McBride presented of a Labour party riven by factions and in-fighting, and more interested in retaining power than governing the country, did him no favours when he was trying to present Labour as a united political force deserving of the voters' trust. But, overall, Miliband could be reasonably satisfied; for the most part, the outgoing Labour elite had behaved surprisingly well in their dying of the light.

Neither Nick Clegg nor David Cameron had many worries on the revenge front; the Lib Dems had never been in power, while the Tories had been in opposition for thirteen years. There were no tales to tell. Except one. Ken Clarke had been health and education secretary under Margaret Thatcher and home secretary and chancellor under John Major, and had remained an MP throughout the years of opposition. He was unmistakably one of the last of the big Tory beasts around Westminster and had challenged Cameron for the leadership of the party in 2005. This made him a potential problem.

Clarke was a strong personality, a grandee who received regular invitations to appear on television and radio and had a solid power base within certain sections of the party. But he was old school: a slightly louche character, who smoked a lot – he had been a director of British American Tobacco while in opposition – wore Hush Puppies and was very much his own man. The very opposite of the new modern Tory image that Cameron was trying to present. Clarke was also a committed Europhile, which was an additional problem at a time when Cameron was trying to stop the more Eurosceptic wing of the Conservative party from moving to Ukip. He was a politician who needed handling with care and Cameron did so in textbook fashion.

For the first two years Clarke was given the Cabinet post of justice secretary; an important role, but not one at the cutting edge of the government. It was a position in which he would be bound by loyalty but could do little harm, and yet also one which Cameron could justifiably claim was proof of his willingness to maintain continuity and the value he placed on experience. Two years into government, Cameron could afford to nudge him a little nearer to the exit and in the 2012 reshuffle he downgraded Clarke to minister without portfolio; still a Cabinet minister, but one whose role was increasingly nebulous. On the few occasions he ventured into the House of Commons, he appeared disengaged, as if he wasn't entirely sure what he was meant to be doing either. He seldom spoke and usually sat alone, all his old friends and colleagues having long since left the building. It was probably as big a relief to him as it was to the prime minister when he was returned to the back benches in the 2014 reshuffle. Cameron had timed cutting the last link with the past perfectly. The Tory party fighting the next election would be in his image and there was little prospect of any comeback. He had let Clarke down gently, and even if his former minister did decide to play rough in a memoir, there wasn't much chance of it getting into print before the election.

Then Cameron took his eye off the ball. Just when he thought he had his front-bench team all lined up to take the Tories into a prolonged election campaign, in August 2014 Baroness Warsi resigned from her Cabinet post as senior minister of state for foreign and commonwealth affairs. Her resignation was sparked by her disagreement with the government over its handling of the conflict between Israel and Gaza – in particular its refusal to condemn Israel; but there was more to it than that. Warsi felt isolated in Cabinet, a lone Asian Muslim female voice who was frequently ignored by a cabal of middle-class white men. True, she had a reputation for being a divisive character. She hadn't been elected to parliament in 2005, and there were some within the Tory party who felt that her subsequent elevation to the House of Lords, chairmanship of the party and appointment to Cabinet had as much to do with her gender, colour and religion as with talent. But there weren't many Asian Muslim women in political life and fewer still with a Tory voice: such a woman needed to be nurtured. Cameron failed to do so sufficiently. Within days of her resignation, he began to suffer the consequences when Warsi extended her criticism of the Tory party to include its appeal to ethnic minorities. The party couldn't win the next election, she said, because it didn't listen to black, working-class voices, and she dismissed her former Cabinet colleagues as the bitchiest people she had ever known.

Warsi didn't come out of this particularly well herself; moving so swiftly from Gaza to personal issues rather devalued the stance she had taken in resigning and, if she had felt that way about the Tories in government, why hadn't she mentioned it before – if only to other colleagues? Even so, Cameron was in a no-win situation. He couldn't just say it was untrue and that Warsi had been love-bombed in Cabinet, because it was just his word against hers and he had no experience of what it was like to be an Asian Muslim woman. He also could have done without someone reminding the British people that the policies for an inclusive 'Big

Society' were being largely thought up by a small elite who wouldn't have to suffer any of the consequences if they went wrong.

August 2014 was not turning out to be the relaxing month off that Cameron had had in mind. As well as the Israel–Gaza crisis and Warsi's resignation, there were on-going tensions in eastern Ukraine and a humanitarian crisis developing in Iraq, where Muslim fundamentalists were threatening the genocide of the Yazidi community in the north-west of the country. There were suggestions that parliament should be recalled, but there wasn't much that could have been achieved by this:

Parliament: So we're back. What next?

Cameron: I think we should condemn the Yazidi genocide.

Parliament: Fair enough. We condemn it. Do you think we should send armed forces there?

Cameron: The last time we sent troops to Iraq didn't turn out so well. So perhaps not. Though we could say that if people don't start behaving we'll send our aircraft carrier to the Gulf when it's finally in service in 2020.

Parliament: All being well. And what about Israel?

Cameron: That's a bit tricky, isn't it? We don't want to upset the Israelis, as they are our friends, so it's probably best if we do very little. Maybe talk a bit. Or suggest someone else talks a bit.

Parliament: Is that it?

Cameron: Pretty much.

So Cameron remained on a beach in Portugal trying to enjoy his holiday. It wasn't easy. Only a few months earlier everything had looked as if it might be falling into place: the economy had started to recover, Labour was questioning Miliband's credentials as leader, and the Conservatives had looked like a united body. Now everything was threatening to unravel. Senior economists were beginning to question just how much the recovery had filtered down to all sections of society; the opinion polls still showed the Conservatives lagging behind Labour; and the Tories had started to do their in-fighting in public. Then along came Boris and everything got even worse for Cameron.

Chapter 16

Boris the Spider

AT 12PM ON EVERY WEDNESDAY THAT PARLIAMENT SITS, THE prime minister and the leader of the opposition go head to head in the half-hour session of Prime Minister's Questions (PMQs); it is the one time fixed into the weekly schedule when the prime minister has to answer to his opposite number in the House of Commons. PMQs used to take place in two fifteen-minute sessions on a Tuesday and Thursday, but Tony Blair ended that in 1997. He preferred to keep his visits to the Commons to a minimum and adjusted the schedule to suit himself.

Every prime minister initially finds PMQs an ordeal. The leader of the opposition is not obliged to give any warning of what questions will be asked and the exchanges always take place before a packed House and almost invariably make the lunchtime news bulletins. Any slip-ups or hesitations are seized on by the opposition and the media. PMQs are as much a game as a question-and-answer session; the prime minister will try to second-guess what the leader of the opposition is going to say and, if taken by surprise, will ad lib before steering the answer round to a pre-prepared reply that can be adapted to fit any question. Hence the government's fondness for dropping leitmotifs, such as 'long-term economic plan', into any sentence. In PMQs, stalling for time while sounding coherent is every bit as important as answering the question. Sometimes more so. The leader of the opposition is allowed only six questions and, when these have been asked, the prime minister is off the hook for the week.

As with most games, it takes practice to get good at PMQs and in the early years of the Coalition Cameron sometimes struggled. He would get angry, red-faced and sound squeaky and brittle when challenged, often becoming the embodiment of the public-school bully – the very thing he was trying to avoid. Whenever this happened, Labour chalked it up as a minor victory. But gradually Cameron got better: he was less fazed by the unexpected, he learned to improvise more skilfully and to keep his emotions and his red face better in check. If asked about longer waiting times in Accident and Emergency, he would simply reply by saying that waiting times for cancer treatment were going down. It wasn't the answer to the question asked; it wasn't even necessarily a correct answer to a different question, as government statistics are notoriously pliable; but it was an answer to a question and Cameron could make it sound plausible. One down, five to go. Next, please.

Miliband, though, was unable to up his game. Never a natural orator, he frequently looked awkward and hesitant as he failed to capitalize on any advantage. Often he didn't appear to know whether to waste another question pointing out that his original one hadn't been answered or to plough on with the next one he had planned to ask. By 2014, PMQs had turned into a rather one-sided affair. The sessions that Miliband ought to have won easily, such as the one following Andy Coulson's conviction, ended in a draw, while Cameron came out of the others comfortably ahead on points and politically unscathed. This placed him in unfamiliar territory. Prime ministers generally have most to fear from the opposition, but neither Labour nor Miliband held many terrors for Cameron; even when wrong-footed by events, he felt secure inside the Commons.

Unusually for a prime minister, all Cameron's biggest headaches were outside Westminster. The most painful of them was to be found lurking in the office of the London mayor. In background, Boris Johnson was almost identical to Cameron; in personality he was the opposite. Johnson was also Eton- and Oxford-educated and had been a member of the Bullingdon Club, yet where these things all counted against Cameron in voters' minds, they were cheerfully and willingly forgiven in Boris.

Boris was different. He was funny and relaxed. He had scruffy hair and he bumbled a bit. He was Boris. No other politician was so readily identified by just his first name. Nor did the public care that much if the Boris they saw was pure artifice. They knew he went out of his way to make sure his hair looked messy when he was out in public. They knew he took himself far more seriously than he liked to suggest. He was allowed to break rules that other politicians weren't. He could make promises he had no intention of keeping, without ever being held to account. He could tirelessly promote himself, and people would enjoy the show-boating. The public knew Boris wasn't really a bumbler and that behind the carapace of confusion was a very bright man, but he got away with it because he had something few other politicians had: natural charm and charisma. What was hidden, though, was the extent of his ambition. Like Cameron, Johnson had had his eye on leading the Tory party since leaving Oxford University.

Johnson entered the House of Commons in 2001, at the same time as David Cameron, though his selection for the safe seat of Henley was not without some duplicity. At the time he was the editor of the weekly magazine the *Spectator* and had promised its owner, Conrad Black, that he wouldn't stand for parliament while he was still working there. That promise was forgotten within months: Boris had no trouble forgiving himself for going back on his word and nor did the public. Most politicians specialize in dreariness; Johnson traded in gaiety. Parliament would be a lot more fun to observe with him inside it.

It was Boris who attracted the attention of the senior Tories in Westminster ahead of Cameron. Within a couple of years he had been appointed vice-chairman of the party and within three he was shadow minister for culture. Within four he had returned to the back benches after Michael Howard, the Conservative leader at the time, fired him for lying to him about an ongoing extra-marital affair with another *Spectator* journalist. This was enough to let Cameron squeeze through the railings and win the Tory party leadership. Cameron immediately asked Johnson to be his shadow education minister, though this was less a display of magnanimity than a tactical necessity. Not only was Johnson's popularity undiminished, but Boris on the back benches was potentially more dangerous than Boris on the front bench, where a minimal level of loyalty could be expected. Even on the front bench Johnson needed to be watched closely, as he continued to defy all the standard political rules.

A year after he became shadow education minister, the *News of the World* ran a story alleging that Johnson was having an affair with an education journalist. One affair has been enough to undermine most political careers. David Mellor never recovered from his, David Blunkett and John Prescott both became targets of humour for theirs, while many people's first thought about John Major is Edwina Currie. Yet Johnson had two affairs and his stature only seemed to increase. People who would condemn other politicians for their infidelity thought Boris was a 'top bloke' for his. It didn't stop at two. Johnson went for the hat trick in 2009 and had an affair with an art consultant from which he emerged as the father of another daughter. Again, he survived the exposure unscathed.

By this time, Johnson had left parliament to become London mayor in 2008. For Cameron, this was a relief. The London mayor was eligible to stand for two four-year terms, so there was little chance of Johnson inflicting much harm until 2016, as only sitting MPs could stand for the leadership of the Tory party. Out of sight wasn't quite out of mind, though: Boris was too big a self-publicist for that. And too ambitious.

He was never coy about his ambitions. The disingenuity was in his intentions. When asked about his desire to be leader of the party, he nearly always replied that of course he would like to do so if the chance arose, but that there was 'more chance of finding Elvis on Mars' and that David Cameron was doing a perfectly good job. In his campaign to be re-elected London mayor in 2012, he 'vowed to serve his term in full' and insisted that 'keeping that promise cannot be combined with any other political capacity'. A more accurate answer would have been that he was biding his time for the most opportune moment, and in the London Olympics he found the ideal launch pad for his move on the top job.

With the world's media trained on London for two weeks in July and August 2012, Johnson went out of his way to be seen in as many places as possible: in the royal box with the Queen, the prime minister and other political leaders and heads of state; in a cable car with Arnold Schwarzenegger; stranded on a zip-wire above Victoria Park; at the women's beach volleyball in Horse Guards Parade – the athletes were 'glistening like wet otters', he said. Anywhere there was a photo opportunity, Boris was there. The country loved him for it. Everywhere he went, he was cheered. Cameron and Osborne had no chance. They were both asked to present the medals at medal ceremonies: there was near silence for Cameron; Osborne was booed. The contrast in popularity didn't escape anyone.

Over the next two years, Johnson was repeatedly asked if he intended to stand for parliament in 2015. Time and again he insisted he wouldn't and that he planned to see out his time as mayor till 2016. He told one journalist that after stepping down in 2016 he was going to 'take up romantic novels under the pseudonym Rosie M. Banks and try to survive by producing airport bonk busters'; to another he said, 'I have a huge amount of work to do [as mayor]. What I've said about it since I was elected is that I thought it was the last big job I would do in public life, and I stick to that.'

Though not for long. Johnson's issue was one of timing. If he kept to his schedule, he would miss out on a chance to be nominated for a safe seat to replace one of the Tories stand-ing down from parliament at the 2015 election, along with the prospect of being in the mix should a leadership contest ensue after the election. Waiting for a by-election after 2016 or, worse still, the general election of 2020, would put him well behind others, such as George Osborne and Theresa May, who were eyeing up Cameron's job.

In August 2014, Johnson finally placed his cards on the table. He was going to have the best of both worlds. He was going to continue as London mayor till 2016 and he was going to look for a seat in which to stand for parliament in 2015. He said he didn't have any particular constituency in mind, but Uxbridge and South Ruislip looked a likely bet. The sitting MP was standing down, it was a safe seat and it was close to London. Within two weeks, Johnson had confirmed he would be standing for Uxbridge.

Multitasking was never an issue for Boris. In the past he had often combined two or three jobs at the same time, and while mayor he had been a columnist for the *Daily Telegraph* for a reported salary of £250,000 – a sum he had described as 'chicken-feed'. But even by his standards, expecting to be able to fulfil the duties of both the London mayor and a constituency MP seemed optimistic. Each one was meant to be a demanding, full-time job and surely it would be impossible for him to avoid doing one – or both – of them badly. Yet no one questioned him on this, so the following conversation never took place:

Reporter: Why Uxbridge, Boris?
Boris: Because it's there. Between you and me, it looks ghastly. I've always tried to pass through it as quickly as possible on my way out of London to the country. But needs must.

Reporter: And if you are elected, how will you fulfil your duties as an MP?

Boris: Well, obviously I'm going to do as little as possible. I might send my constituency manager up to Uxbridge to do a weekly meet and greet, and I will probably drop into the Commons for PMQs and lunch on Wednesdays, but otherwise I will be busy as mayor.

Reporter: What if there's a leadership contest after the election. Will you stand?

Boris: Are you mad? Of course I will.

Reporter: Who will do your mayor's job then?

Boris: Oh, I don't know. It's not that hard really. You just go out and talk to people about traffic and how wonderful London is. I'm sure the deputy can stand in for me for the last year.

Reporter: Who is the deputy?

Boris: Do you know, I haven't a clue.

Reporter: Will you give up your column on the *Telegraph*?

Boris: For that money?

'Great news that Boris plans to stand at next year's general election – I've always said I want my star players on the pitch,' David Cameron said through gritted teeth from his holiday villa in Portugal. He could sense the vultures circling. He knew that Johnson hadn't announced his come-back on a whim; he had done so after months of meticulous planning with his kitchen Cabinet of senior Tories – an anonymous group the press referred to as 'Friends of Boris' who could be relied on to leak stories in favour of their man and against Cameron. Johnson was coming back because he reckoned he now had the best chance of landing the biggest prize.

There was a small upside to Johnson's return. Boris had a

style that no other politician could match and his presence at the heart of the election campaign could give the Conservatives a much-needed lift in the polls. In August 2014, the Tories were still at least three or four percentage points behind Labour: Johnson could make a big difference, if not in getting the Tory message across to undecided voters, then in charming them. But his return still meant trouble for Cameron. While it had always been likely that anything less than an overall Conservative majority at the 2015 election would have triggered talk of a leadership contest, there was always the possibility that he might have been able to see off the challenge. With Johnson now definitely in the mix, his chances of survival were minimal.

Johnson had little to lose. If the Tories didn't win an overall majority, he would get his chance sooner; if they did, he would have a spell in the Cabinet before making his move later. Many newspapers were reporting Johnson's elevation to party leader and thence to prime minister as virtually a done deal. None, though, was asking what Boris might be like if he did get his hands on the top job. It was something worth thinking about. People enjoy funny, gaffe-prone politicians when they aren't in power: they brighten up the day and make the news fun. But, in power, might a predictable, boring man – or woman – in a suit be a rather better bet than someone who can't be trusted not to sleep with the French president's wife, or who is liable to challenge President Putin to an arm-wrestling match for a laugh?

Reporter: What is your response to Angela Merkel's statement on the euro?
Boris: Well, I'd just like to remind her that Britain has

already seen off the Hun in two world wars and I'm quite happy to take her on again. The bombers are already on their way to Dresden, ha ha!

Reporter: I see. Do you think there's any chance of a rapprochement?

Boris: There's always a chance. Never say never. But she's not much of a looker, so she'll have to work a bit to charm me round the table. Ha ha!

Reporter: Do the North Koreans pose a credible threat to world stability?

Boris: I was talking about this to the Americans only the other day. To be honest, we're both getting a bit fed up with old Kim Jong-un and his cronies holding the world to ransom. One of these days, I'm going to lose my temper and just nuke them. See this button? Boom! Ha ha!

Reporter: Moving on to domestic matters, what do you say to those who argue that the recovery is very uneven and that people in the north of the country are less well off than those in the south?

Boris: There are always going to winners and losers in any situation and I think it's about time the Scousers stopped moaning and got off their large backsides and did a proper day's work. Ha ha!

Reporter: Thank you very much, Prime Minister.

It was hard for anyone to work out what Johnson really believed in and stood for. Except himself. Beyond being an old-school One Nation Tory, Johnson had never seemed to have any policies or ideology. In itself, this wasn't necessarily a bad thing. Ideologues often created more problems than solutions. But there was a fine line between a pragmatic politician who could adapt policy to changing circumstances and an out-and-out opportunist. Johnson had always given the impression of being a politician who stepped well over that line; his statements after announcing he would stand for parliament reinforced that.

Time and again, he sought to put clear blue water between himself and Cameron. As the prime minister struggled to find an appropriate response to the beheading of a US journalist by an Islamic State terrorist thought to be a British citizen, Johnson made hay. Cameron even broke off his surfing holiday in Cornwall and returned to Downing Street for a couple of days, but there was little he could do or say beyond condemning the killing, as he was still hoping to avoid any military action in the Middle East. Johnson had no such responsibility: he could tap into the country's revulsion by saying anyone travelling to Iraq or Syria should be presumed guilty of being a jihadist until proven innocent. It was nothing more than shameless populism and Johnson knew it. Such a change in the law was never on the cards.

Europe, though, was Cameron's weakest spot and Johnson went straight for the jugular there, too, by reeling off a long list of reforms that the European Union would have to make before he would back any plan for Britain to stay in the organization. It didn't matter that some of the reforms he was calling for had already been agreed in principle by all European leaders; what mattered was that he had seized the initiative with a populist stance that was guaranteed to win support from the Eurosceptics.

Johnson had laid down his marker. He was going to continue to be a thorn in the prime minister's side for the foreseeable future. And so would Europe.

Chapter 17

Waterloo

WHEN THE CONSERVATIVE PRIME MINISTER EDWARD HEATH TOOK Britain into the European Economic Community – or Common Market, as the European Union was then known – in 1973, the main opposition came from the left. Within two years, even Labour had come round. There were minor deceptions, of course; no prime minister could afford to be too truthful about exactly how many sovereign powers would be handed over to the European parliament in Brussels. But overall the EEC was looking an increasingly good bet: the French and German economies were growing, while Britain's own economic difficulties had just resulted in a three-day week, and in 1975, when the Labour leader Harold Wilson was prime minister, 67 per cent of the country voted in a referendum to stay in the Common Market.

Within ten years, the pendulum had swung the other way. While the Labour party was by now firmly on board with the European ideal, many in the Conservative government, under Margaret Thatcher, had begun to have second thoughts. In their view, Britain was contributing far too much to the EU budget – Thatcher negotiated a two-thirds rebate – and the main EU countries were being run by social democratic governments that couldn't be trusted because they were all pinkos in disguise. This all chimed well with those sections of the country that had never quite stopped thinking of Germany and France as the enemy and felt that Europe really ended at Calais and the Channel existed primarily to keep everyone else out. Thus was born the division within the Tory party between those who regarded the EU as a benign organization conferring prosperity on all its members and those who suspected its ultimate purpose was to undermine the British sense of identity.

The rift rumbled on within the Tory party throughout the 1990s and the early 2000s without causing too many problems, as the anti-Europeans found themselves squeezed to the margins of the debate. With Labour, the Lib Dems and the mainstream Tories all pro-European, the Eurosceptics inevitably found themselves painted as golf-club Little Englanders or extreme right-wingers – an impression that was reinforced by the fact that the only other political parties to share their ideas were the British National Party (BNP) and the UK Independence Party (Ukip). The BNP was a neo-fascist organization whose support was primarily found in white, working-class urban areas and whose electoral successes had been limited to a few wards in local council elections. Ukip had rather more respectability; its views were less extreme, its membership more middle class, and it had improved its showing at successive European elections. In 1999, it had won 7 per cent of the vote and three seats in the European parliament; in 2004, Ukip had 16 per cent of the vote and 12 seats; by 2009 it had nudged ahead of Labour into second place behind the Conservatives and had 13 MEPs.

But despite this success in the European elections, Ukip was still considered very much a marginal force in domestic politics. The nature of the first-past-the-post electoral system meant that the party didn't really have a chance of winning a single seat in a British election, and many of those who voted Ukip in a European election put their cross against the Tories in a general election. There were two reasons for this: first, Europe had never traditionally been a deciding issue in UK elections; and second, Ukip didn't bear too much scrutiny as a serious political party. Its only truly recognizable politician was Nigel Farage, who had been its leader since 2006 and came across as an amiable, if not particularly bright, sort of bloke you might find in any pub in the Surrey stockbroker belt; indeed, the one place you could almost guarantee *not* to find him, or any of the other Ukip MEPs, was in Brussels. A survey in 2014 revealed that the Ukip MEPs ranked bottom of the seventy-six parties in the European parliament in terms of attendance.

While a few minor public figures, such as former Labour MP and chat-show host Robert Kilroy-Silk, joined the party, their membership tended to be fractious and brief – Kilroy-Silk left within a year of signing up in 2004 – and the impression remained that Ukip was a single-issue party led by a single politician. Even in 2010 Nigel Farage looked as if he would be hard pushed to name a single member of his Shadow Cabinet:

Paxman: So, Mr Farage, in the 2006 Bromley by-election you came third, winning just 8 per cent of the vote. You're now contesting the speaker's seat of Buckingham. What chance do you have of getting elected?

Farage: Um, er, the people will decide . . .

Paxman: Indeed they will. Let's just say for a moment you *do* get elected to parliament. You will then, presumably, be leader of Ukip in parliament?

Farage: Indeed.

Paxman: And who will be your inner circle? Your spokesmen on the economy, foreign affairs and domestic issues?

Farage: That would rather depend on who else was elected at the same time as me.

Paxman: I see. So you will basically have to wait until after the election, see who is around, and divvy up the jobs as best as possible?

Farage: Sounds reasonable.

Paxman: And if there was just one other Ukip MP?

Farage: I think I could manage being party leader and chancellor. And the other person could do everything else. I'm sure we can also rope in a few MEPs to help out. They aren't doing much in Brussels.

Paxman: OK. So we have the personnel sorted out. Can we move on to policy? What exactly is your agenda?

Farage: First and foremost, we want to make sure Britain isn't ruled from Europe. That Britain is free to pursue its own policies without any interference from petty, small-minded European bureaucrats who want to destroy us.

Paxman: How exactly is this going to translate into steering the economy towards recovery and managing schools and the NHS?

Farage: It's all in our 486-page election manifesto, Jeremy.

Paxman: Is it? I'm glad you've brought that up. There were one or two things I wanted to ask you about. It says here that you want to introduce a dress code for taxi drivers. What sort of uniform did you have in mind?

Farage: Er . . .

Paxman: You also want to deploy troops on the streets, re-paint trains in traditional colours, have a proper dress code for the theatre, scrap maternity leave, make the Circle underground line circular again, investigate racism against white people at the BBC, teach schoolchildren about the roles of Arab and African countries in promoting slavery, and reintroduce capital punishment.

Farage: They sounded like good ideas at the time.

Four years later, Farage finally admitted that the Ukip election manifesto for 2010 had basically been a load of nonsense put together by a few party activists and that he himself had never got round to reading it. Yet even though Ukip had by then grown into a slightly slicker, more professional operation than it had been in 2010, it was still prone to shooting itself in the foot far too often. The party simply wasn't big enough or well-organized enough to vet every single one of its members – or for that matter its prospective candidates for local, parliamentary and European elections – and all too often it would find itself in the eye of an embarrassing storm.

In 2013 alone, Ukip repeatedly made headlines for all the wrong reasons. First, a Ukip candidate named Geoffrey Clarke had to be suspended over suggestions in his online manifesto that compulsory abortion should be considered for foetuses with Down's syndrome or spina bifida. Then, on a Ukip online forum, another of the party's candidates allegedly described gay sex as 'disgusting' and said homosexuals were not 'normal'; in response, Nigel Farage said he would not expel members for voicing 'old-fashioned' views about homosexuality. Days later, the chairman of Ukip's youth wing was sacked after speaking out in favour of gay marriage.

That was just the start. Another Ukip candidate, Alex Wood, was caught on camera making what appeared to be a Nazi salute; a Ukip donor, Demetri Marchessini, said it was 'hostile' of women to wear trousers rather than skirts; and a *Sunday Mirror* investigation revealed that Chris Pain, Ukip's East Midlands chairman and a Lincoln councillor, had described illegal immigrants as 'sandal-wearing, bomb-making, camel-riding, goat-fucking ragheads' on his Facebook page, though he later claimed his account had been hacked. By way of a *pièce de résistance*, MEP Godfrey Bloom was filmed saying Britain should not send aid to 'Bongo Bongo Land', claiming the recipients spent the money on 'Ray-Ban sunglasses, apartments in Paris, Ferraris and all the rest of it'. He followed this up by shouting 'This place is full of sluts' at an event to promote women's participation in politics.

By 2014, little had improved. In January, an Oxfordshire councillor, David Silvester, blamed the flooding that submerged large parts of the UK that winter on the government's decision to legalize gay marriage. The following month Gerard Batten, a founding member of Ukip, called for Muslims to be made to sign a special 'code of conduct'. Soon after, Roger Helmer, an MEP and prospective candidate in the Newark by-election, suggested that heterosexuality was morally preferable to homosexuality. In August, MEP Janice Atkinson was forced to apologize after calling a Thai Ukip supporter a 'ting tong'.

The prevailing impression was of a party more or less out of control, with no one really having much idea what anyone else was doing, and with political gaffes and casual racism and sexism everyday occurrences. It was an image Farage did little to dispel. Much of his popularity was centred around the fact that he wasn't a polished, professional politician like the leaders of the other parties. He was just an ordinary bloke who enjoyed a few pints – he sometimes arranged for his media interviews to take place in pubs – and voiced the concerns of the ordinary man in the street. If he got the odd thing wrong, or if one of his supporters said something a bit out of line, it was just one of those things. No one meant any harm by it. Besides, wouldn't you rather have a party where people were free to say what they liked than one in which everyone was expected always to be on message?

It turned out that this was precisely the sort of party that more and more people did want. Though part of its appeal was located in its common touch and in a disillusionment with mainstream Westminster politics, Ukip's message also had an economic resonance for some voters. The economy had tanked on Labour's watch and had failed to improve much on the Coalition's; the three main parties were all considered to be equally bad and only in it for themselves. The country was being stitched up by a small metropolitan elite, the bankers and the politicians in Brussels; meanwhile, the ordinary person was being squeezed out.

At the heart of this was a fear that something quintessentially British was being lost and that the country was no longer recognizably the one people had known even just twenty years earlier. This was not an entirely misplaced fear. A Home Office report in 2003 had forecast that the impact of the enlargement of the EU would result in only 5,000–13,000 nationals from former Eastern European countries per year taking advantage of the freedom of movement laws to come to Britain; in 2011, however, 168,000 long-term migrants came to the UK from within the EU. For Ukip this was proof that the system had failed; the floodgates had opened and hundreds of thousands of poor people who couldn't find work in their own countries had come to scrounge off the largesse of Britain.

Neither, though, was Ukip's vision of Britain being overrun by Eastern Europeans entirely accurate. Although 1.5 million migrants had come to the UK from Europe since 2004, 644,000 people had also left. Nor was there any evidence that the Eastern Europeans had come to claim benefits from the British welfare system; quite the reverse, in fact, as EU migrants made fewer benefit claims per capita than British people. The large majority of migrants had come to work and were doing building or agricultural jobs for significantly lower wages than their British counterparts; their British employers had been overjoyed by their arrival. Nor had Britain been targeted by EU migrants as an especially easy touch; as a proportion of population, the UK had taken in fewer foreigners than eleven other EU countries.

These nuances seldom featured in any Ukip argument about Europe, though. The only message the party had about the EU was that it was a poison eating away at British life. It was sucking money and jobs out of the country, destroying British culture and diminishing our sovereignty; left to its own devices, the EU would force Britain into a European super-state and prevent us from making our own laws. Dozens of EU laws already took precedence over British law in some areas, and if we weren't careful it wouldn't be long before the rest were superseded too. Before we knew it, we'd be wearing berets and lederhosen, driving on the right-hand side of the road and our currency would have been converted to the euro. What was needed, Ukip said, was another referendum: the British electorate should be allowed to have their say on whether or not they wanted to remain in the EU. What's more, a significant number of British people now agreed that this was an entirely reasonable demand.

A referendum on the EU was the last thing Cameron and Clegg – or even Miliband, for that matter – wanted. The fundamental purpose of the House of Commons is to take difficult decisions on behalf of the country. A referendum always holds out the possibility of politicians being forced to take action when they would rather do nothing. If the Coalition were to grant a referendum on capital punishment, there's a fair chance there would be a gallows on every street corner within a matter of years. And a referendum on Europe raised the very real possibility that Britain might have to leave the EU, which was the last thing any of the three party leaders wanted. The EU might have its annoyances, but as a trading organization it worked reasonably well, and a Britain outside it would be isolated. Also, any British prime minister who took the country out of Europe would be marginalized by all the other European leaders.

As long as Ukip had no real political power base in the UK, the Westminster politicians needed to do little but pay lip-service to the idea of a referendum. Sometimes they didn't even bother to pay lip-service. In 2006 David Cameron described Ukip members as 'fruitcakes, loonies and closet racists'; other MPs later made references to Ukip's

MEPs milking the Brussels expenses system and rarely turning up to vote. It wasn't long, however, before everyone had to soften the message considerably. Although in February 2013 the Lib Dems held the Eastleigh by-election that followed Chris Huhne's resignation, just three months later Ukip made significant gains in the mid-term local elections, while the Lib Dems suffered heavy losses. Ukip had grown from being a small party of protest voters into something far more politically significant. It no longer merely drew its support from disaffected right-wing Tories; it also had a hold among the Labour-voting, white working class that felt its party had become too metropolitan and middle class. While Ukip was still some way short of being a threat in a general election, there was now the possibility that it might one day become one. Westminster had had a nasty shock in 2010 when it discovered the two-party system had become a three-party one; now they wanted to avoid the further shock of three parties becoming four.

The most pressing concern at the beginning of 2014 was the European elections that were coming up in May. The opinion polls gave Ukip a big lead and there seemed little chance of any of the other parties overhauling it. A change of tactics was required. Rather than ignoring or downplaying Ukip's concerns, Cameron was now obliged to take them seriously as support for Ukip was taking hold within his own party and he wanted to limit the number of voters defecting to Ukip at the general election in a year's time. It was often an uneasy balancing act. While he had now conceded a referendum on Europe, he had promised it would take place some time well after the general election – by which time he would have renegotiated a better deal. He hoped.

Ukip: We want a referendum now.

Cameron: You can't have one.

Ukip: Why not?

Cameron: Because it's too soon and there's a danger you might win. And even if you don't, you will have hijacked the terms of the debate going into the general election.

Ukip: And your plan is?

Cameron: I am going to spend a lot of time chatting to other European leaders about how we can change the EU constitution in small but important cosmetic ways in order to make Britain more autonomous. Then we can have a referendum. There's no point in having one before that, is there?

Ukip: When will these negotiations have been completed?

Cameron: That's a tricky one. These conversations can be very delicate.

Ukip: Roughly, though?

Cameron: I was thinking of some time that isn't so far away that it sounds as if I'm fobbing you off, and one that isn't so near as to make life difficult right now.

Ukip: So 2017 then?

Cameron: That sounds about right.

The most obvious outward sign that Ukip was being taken more seriously was the invitation extended in spring 2014 by LBC Radio and the BBC for Farage to participate in two leaders' debates ahead of the European elections. Previously, Ukip had been considered too much of a minority interest group to join a debate. Sensibly, both Cameron and Miliband realized the best way to limit any damage that might result from going head to head with Farage was to decline to take part. Just as the leaders' debates before the general election in 2010 had raised Clegg's profile significantly, so this one would give Farage a bigger platform. The public's sympathy would inevitably tend to lie with the outsider rather than with anyone from the Westminster establishment.

Nick Clegg, though, agreed to take part. In some ways he had little to lose; both his personal and his party's popularity ratings were at an all-time low and, as the Lib Dems were the one party to embrace the EU unreservedly, if he wasn't prepared to defend Europe in a public debate then it would look as if there was no one from the centre of government who was willing to do so. In the end, neither Farage nor Clegg covered themselves with glory.

In the first debate, Farage won merely by dint of appearing slightly the more human of the two: not that the benchmark of humanity was particularly high. Ahead of round two, Clegg announced he was going to do his best to come across as more personable. This didn't seem the sharpest of moves; telling your audience that you are going to pull out all the stops to be likeable doesn't encourage a belief that this is something that comes naturally.

The second debate began as a series of pre-scripted, undercooked gags. Farage made a joke about the presenter, David Dimbleby, and Clegg followed up with 'Billy-no-mates Britain, Billy-no-jobs Britain' and 'I'm the leader of In. He's the leader of Putin.' Nobody in the audience laughed. Thereafter, the debate went back and forth like a tame pub brawl: Farage maintained that the whole of Europe was about to fall under the EU jackboot and that the whole continent was going to become a 485-million-strong standing army; Clegg insisted the EU was basically no bigger than the total number of people employed by Derbyshire county council, and that if we left the EU we would have no control over telephone roaming charges when we went on holiday abroad. The only consensus came when Clegg promised that everyone coming into Britain in the future would be made to learn English: this was a vision of the green and pleasant land Nigel could live with.

'I'm not sure if that made things any clearer,' Dimbleby said ruefully when the hour was up. Nor was anyone else. Farage had claimed that 70 per cent of British laws were made in Europe, while Clegg declared it was only 7 per cent. Neither gave way and there was no possibility of knowing who was right, nor what level of draconian law-making was being invoked. Was the jackboot of Europe forcing Britain to standardize its ice-cream cones to a maximum diameter of five centimetres? Who knew? If Farage or Clegg did, they weren't saying.

The most immediate observable fallout from the two debates was in the ratings of the two parties. Clegg had failed to boost his own party's support, while Ukip continued to get a free ride from the public. Farage was like a less clever version of Boris Johnson: both were granted political immunity because they were funny and the public liked them. As with Johnson, Farage got away with things that would have destroyed other politicians. During the campaign for the European elections, he declared that Romanians were far more likely to commit crime than British people and that many wouldn't want Romanians moving in next door to them for that reason; at a time when Farage was trying to reinvent Ukip as a credible party of opposition to Europe rather than a collection of disaffected British people who didn't like foreigners, it was a serious own goal. But still it did him no harm with the electorate. Come the May elections, Ukip had the biggest share of the vote, with 26.6 per cent. Labour came second with 24.4 per cent and the Conservatives third with 23 per cent. The Lib Dems were reduced to 6.6 per cent of the vote and just one representative in the European parliament.

The Newark by-election that took place on the same day as the European elections ran more to form. Although the by-election had been made necessary when the Tory MP Patrick Mercer stood down after being exposed by the *Daily Telegraph* and BBC's *Panorama* for accepting cash payments in return for asking questions on behalf of lobbying groups – Mercer had developed a sudden interest in all matters relating to Fiji – the Newark voters were in no mood to punish the Conservatives for another sleaze episode and they elected the fresh-faced Tory candidate Robert Jenrick as his replacement. Despite large numbers of Ukip activists on the ground – including former disgraced Tory MP, turned TV minor celeb, turned Ukip campaign director Neil Hamilton – their candidate, the latter-day Basil Fawlty lookalike Roger 'Don't tell anyone, but I think my hat is Swedish' Helmer, was well beaten into second place. The Tories put up a tough fight, with every Cabinet minister under instruction to visit the constituency three times during the election campaign. Labour also sent its A-list MPs to Newark, though more to ensure it wasn't embarrassed at the polls than in expectation of winning the seat. The Lib Dems were all but wiped out. Three days before the election their candidate, David Watts, was walking disconsolately through the market square when several people rushed past him. 'Those are my colleagues,' he said. 'Even they are avoiding me.'

Holding Newark did at least give Cameron some breathing space. It showed that British voters still didn't trust Ukip in domestic matters. Perhaps wisely. Before the by-election Helmer had been asked about his party's plans for the economy. 'I can't tell you what our economic policy is,' he had replied, 'because we haven't published it yet.' It was an honest answer, if not one to inspire confidence. But the European election results were still a headache. Cameron might at one time have hoped that once these elections were over Europe could revert to his preferred place for it: the back burner. This was now no longer a viable option. While some of Ukip's more exuberant supporters interpreted the 2014 election results as a sign that the party might win 12–15 seats at the 2015 general election and possibly even hold the balance of power, the more realistic – and still extremely damaging – outcome was that the rise in support for Ukip could split the Conservative vote in key constituencies and allow Labour in through the back door.

To minimize the chances of this happening, Cameron needed to take a more adversarial approach towards Europe in order to keep the more Eurosceptical wing of his own party happy. Where previously he had adopted a more cautious tone in his advocacy of EU reform, highlighting the benefits of membership and the dangers of isolation if Britain left, he now went more strongly on the attack. If the EU wasn't prepared to make radical changes to its constitution in order to give Britain – and other countries – more autonomy, then there would be a referendum and he, David Cameron, couldn't be held responsible for the result. The Conservative Europhiles bit the bullet and kept quiet, understanding that preventing further defections to Ukip was more important than ideology. The Lib Dems, the most fervent of pro-Europeans, were left high and dry. The Coalition, which had come into existence four years earlier in a fanfare of goodwill as a new way of doing politics that transcended party interests, had again been exposed as an expedient shell. When the chips were down, tribal politics won every time. It was becoming harder and harder to find anything on which the two parties agreed, other than that they both preferred being in power to being out of it.

It wasn't just Britain that had shown a profound scepticism towards EU membership in the European elections. France, Denmark and Greece had all recorded a significant increase in support for far-right nationalist parties, and with many EU countries still struggling to recover from the global economic recession, the mood was shifting. The poorest countries within the Eurozone had begun to take issue with the austerity measures being dictated to them by the most economically successful – principally Germany – and there was a feeling in many quarters that the balance of control had shifted too far away from national sovereignty towards a centralized European bureaucracy. Even the most committed of EU politicians privately accepted that some change was required if the discontent was to be contained: any country deciding to leave the EU would cause almost as many complications for those that remained as it did for itself in going it alone. Would one departure spark others? What would any new terms of engagement involve?

The new, more Eurosceptic Cameron, though, didn't feel an entirely natural construction. Left to his own instincts, he might have been more effective in the negotiations to re-draw EU powers. As with most things connected with Europe, there were protocols to be observed. Negotiations couldn't be rushed and politicians and countries couldn't be seen to lose face. This, however, was a style Cameron could no longer afford after Ukip's success in the European elections. He needed to demonstrate his antagonism to Europe in public, and a month after the elections he went in with all guns blazing over the appointment of the new president of the European Commission, whom he did not believe was the right man to oversee the reform of the EU:

Cameron: I will not be rail-roaded into accepting the nomination of Jean-Claude Juncker as the next president.

10 other EU leaders: Ssshh . . .

Cameron: I said, 'I will not be rail-roaded into accepting the nomination of Jean-Claude Juncker as the next president.'

10 other EU leaders: Not so loud. That's not how we do things here. We think he's too much of an insider too. But these matters need to be handled delicately.

Cameron: Isn't anyone listening? I said, 'I will not be rail-roaded into accepting the nomination of Jean-Claude Juncker as the next president.'

10 other EU leaders: Fine. Have it your own way, then. But now we'll all have to vote against you.

Hungary: We're still with you!

Juncker: And the final vote is twenty-six in favour of me and two against. I win!

Miliband: You've just humiliated yourself, Prime Minister.

Cameron: The Hungarians have always been our most important ally in Europe.

Miliband: They are now . . .

Cameron: I may have been outvoted, but I believe in sticking up for my principles.

The principle at stake wasn't a more transparent election of the next European Commission, though: it was securing Cameron's power base for the next election at home. And in the short term it was cost-effective: being so hopelessly out-numbered in the vote was a price worth paying for keeping the Eurosceptics in his party happy. The long term was less certain. Within the EU, Cameron's tactics had put other leaders' backs up and so their willingness to negotiate favourably at a later date on changes to Britain's membership conditions had been compromised. If, as Cameron had always maintained, he wanted Britain to remain in the EU, he had just made his life a little harder. That, though, was a second-order problem. First and foremost, he had to win the general election in 2015.

Nor was Miliband immune to the Ukip effect. Support for the party among disenchanted Labour voters – particularly from the north of the country – continued to grow, and however much Labour strategists might reckon these voters would return to the fold in May 2015, Miliband couldn't be seen to be taking their support for granted. So he, too, started to up his game with increasingly anti-European rhetoric, along with promises of a crackdown on people coming into Britain and a tougher welfare system. It wasn't a traditionally Labour message by any means and Miliband seldom sounded convincing when selling it.

All of which made for an almost surreal European interlude in the lead-up to the election. The Lib Dems scarcely dared mention the EU because doing so risked eroding their support still further, while both Cameron and Miliband were being edged towards positions that many voters instinctively recognized they didn't really believe in. Cameron also had the added problem of Boris Johnson, who was missing few opportunities to turn up the heat with anti-European rhetoric of his own. Before long, though, even Boris was a minor issue.

In late August, Nigel Farage confirmed what many had already suspected: he would be standing as a Ukip candidate for Thanet in Kent at the 2015 election and his party would be contesting eight other Conservative-held seats. The threat had become real. A few days later, Cameron's other fear was realized as Douglas Carswell announced he was joining Ukip and would be standing down as the Conservative MP for Clacton in Essex. The principal reason Carswell gave for his defection was that he no longer trusted Cameron's promises on EU reform; to add insult to injury, on the same day the Office for National Statistics released figures showing that immigration had gone up by more than 36 per cent to 243,000 in the previous year. Cameron's pledge to reduce immigration to 100,000 per year by 2015 looked to be in tatters.

There would now be a by-election in early October in which Carswell would stand for Ukip against a Tory candidate. Clacton was precisely the sort of constituency that Ukip wanted to target – white, working class, with a relatively high Eastern European immigrant community – and Farage made the most of his party's PR coup by letting the media know that eight Eurosceptic MPs had had lunch with Ukip party chairman Stuart Wheeler, and that further defections were imminent. Several prominent Eurosceptic

MPs immediately made public pledges of loyalty to David Cameron, but as MPs aren't always noted for keeping their word, the speculation escalated.

How this would all play out was anyone's guess. Though the opinion polls gave him a strong lead there was no certainty Carswell would become Ukip's first MP. He might have held a 12,000 majority at the 2010 election, but there would be a large number of Conservative voters who would stick with the party rather than follow Carswell to Ukip. Had Carswell's defection forced Cameron's hand, or had he made it harder for Eurosceptics within the Tories to get their own way? Would more defections follow or was Carswell a lone wolf? No one knew. Just when Cameron most wanted to keep his party on a tight leash, he had been forced on to the defensive.

There was some let-up, though. For a short period in September these worries could go temporarily on hold, as the most immediate political minefield had moved from Brussels to several hundred miles north of Westminster.

Chapter 18

I Would Walk 500 Miles

ALMOST A YEAR TO THE DAY AFTER THE UK GENERAL ELECTION
of 2010, voters returned a Scottish National Party (SNP)
majority government to the Scottish parliament for the first
time. Under its existing powers, which had been devolved
from Westminster in 1999, the Scottish Assembly was able to
legislate only on 'unreserved' matters, such as health and
education; 'reserved' powers, including sovereignty, fiscal
and monetary policy, energy and international affairs,
remained under the control of Westminster. Central to the
SNP's election manifesto, both in 2007 and in 2011, was that
a referendum should be held on Scottish independence. This
was something no one at Westminster much wanted to give
– indeed there were many in parliament who felt that devolution to Scotland, Wales and Northern Ireland had already
gone quite far enough – but with the SNP having won a
majority, it was now hard to refuse.

For Alex Salmond, leader of the SNP since 2004 and
Scottish first minister since 2007, the British government's
agreement to a referendum was a moment of both triumph
and possible disaster. A triumph because he had backed
the politicians in Westminster into a corner where denying a

referendum would appear undemocratic; a possible disaster because he was by no means certain that most Scottish voters wanted to be independent of the UK and break up the union that had existed since 1707. While many Scots had no great love for England or the English – a feeling that had intensified during the 1980s, when many north of the border believed that Margaret Thatcher's government had destroyed Scottish industry and channelled North Sea oil profits to England – there was still a natural in-built reluctance to rock the boat; it was the difference between sticking two fingers up to Westminster as an outsider when there was little at stake and voting to change the entire constitutional and economic framework.

Much as he would have hated the comparison, Salmond was now in a similar situation to the one Nick Clegg had found himself in a year earlier. His bluff had been called and his demands on Westminster were being taken seriously: his career was on the line. Almost immediately, he appeared to backtrack:

Salmond: You know when I said I wanted Scottish independence?
Cameron: It was hard to avoid . . .
Salmond: What I was really talking about was devolution max.
Cameron: Sorry? Then why have you always gone on and on about independence?
Salmond: Because I never thought we'd get a referendum.
Cameron: So what do you suggest?
Salmond: How about we have three questions on the referendum ballot? Yes to independence; no to independence; and

243

let's forget about independence and give Scotland loads more executive and fiscal powers? What do you reckon?

Cameron: I'll chat about it to George Osborne. George – three questions or two?

Osborne: Definitely two.

Salmond: Why?

Osborne: Because we've seen the opinion polls and we don't think you've got a cat in hell's chance of getting a Yes vote. But if we included devo max, most Scots would vote for it and you'd be off the hook. This referendum isn't just about killing off any talk of independence for the immediate future, it's about killing off your career. To be blunt, no one at Westminster has ever much liked you and no one would be sorry if we didn't have to hear from you ever again.

Salmond did manage to negotiate two concessions. He had the voting age for the referendum lowered from eighteen to sixteen, correctly believing that younger voters would be more likely to be in favour of independence; and he was able to choose the wording of the questions on the ballot paper so that a vote for independence was a 'Yes' vote. Undecided voters have been shown to be more likely to choose the option with the most positive message.

With the details hammered out, the Scottish referendum was largely forgotten south of the border. It was a long way off, there were a lot of other issues that were a great deal more pressing and everyone thought the result was a done deal. The Scots would never vote to break up the Union, so why waste time thinking about it? Apart from anything else, one of the key irritants for the Scottish Nationalists was excessive interference from Westminster, so many politicians reckoned that appearing to get involved would be counter-productive. Far better just to let the Scots get on with things and come to the right decision by themselves.

There's a difference between not getting involved and being complacent, though. And all the parties got the balance wrong. The Tories, at least, had an excuse. The Conservative brand in Scotland was fairly toxic and almost any intervention they made was bound to add votes to the Yes campaign. Added to this, there was a possible upside to Scottish independence for them. Although the full title of the Conservative party is the Conservative and Unionist party and many Tories would, in the short term, find it hard to forgive Cameron for losing Scotland, they might have come to appreciate some of the electoral benefits. In 2010, the Conservatives won only one Scottish seat in Westminster. Labour, though, had forty Scottish MPs and, were Scotland to go independent, it would lose them all within a year and would struggle to form a majority government thereafter.

Electoral advantage in Westminster wasn't the only reason the Labour party should have campaigned in Scotland. Like many nationalist parties, the SNP had begun life as a fairly right-wing, reactionary organization that drew its support from disaffected, conservative-minded voters; the more progressive, working-class population in Scotland tended to be hard-line Labour voters. The Labour party, though, took its working-class supporters for granted, confident they would vote as they always had done, and with this assumption Labour played into the hands of the SNP and the independence movement. Telling people they are being ignored is never a particularly hard sell when it happens to be true.

Little by little, the independence campaign gained in strength and by the early months of 2014 had become a mass popular movement.

Even when the opinion polls started indicating the gap between the No and Yes camps had narrowed to 60–40, there were few signs of panic in Westminster. The expert pollsters insisted referenda were very different animals to general elections and that the 'Don't Knows' invariably voted in favour of the status quo, so there was nothing much to worry about. It was all a storm in a teacup and everything would turn out right in the end; but, just to make sure, the No campaign upped its game a little. The author J. K. Rowling donated £1million to make sure there were plenty of adverts warning of the dangers of independence, and Westminster politicians sounded off about the dire economic consequences of a split. Scotland wouldn't be able to use sterling as its currency and all its banks and financial institutions would have to relocate to London.

The tactics initially appeared to be working. In the first televised debate between Alex Salmond and Alistair Darling, held in early August 2014, Darling, the former Labour chancellor who had been delegated to run the No campaign, got the upper hand:

Darling: If Scotland goes independent, you won't be able to use the pound.
Salmond: Yes we can.
Darling: No you can't. It's not down to you. It's our pound and you can't have it.
Salmond: Yes we can.
Darling: No you can't. George Osborne says you can't, the

Treasury says you can't and all the financial institutions say you can't.

Salmond: Well, I say I can. We'll just print notes that say 'pound' on them and you can't stop us.

Darling: But they won't be worth anything.

Salmond: They will to me. They will be worth their weight in votes.

Darling: But you have to have a Plan B in case it turns out you can't use the pound. What is your Plan B?

Salmond: Plan A.

Darling: Sorry?

Salmond: Plan A is my Plan B.

Darling: So what is your Plan A?

Salmond: Are you deliberately trying to be stupid? My Plan A is my Plan A.

The lack of clarity on any of the main issues seemed to be decisive. No one really knew either what the constitutional make-up of an independent Scotland would be, how it would engage economically with the rest of the UK or whether it would be part of the EU, because no one had reckoned it was worth thinking through. Why bother to waste time on such tricky problems when they were so obviously not going to materialize? Furthermore, with no concrete answers to any of these matters, Westminster politicians thought it inevitable that Scottish voters would pull back. Romanticism would give way to pragmatism.

Many of the Scots saw it differently, though. They weren't that concerned about the economic and constitutional realities of a post-independence Scotland. They saw they had been given a once-in-a-lifetime opportunity to change the face of Scottish politics and they didn't feel like wasting it. They didn't necessarily all believe in Alex Salmond's rose-tinted visions of £50 notes floating towards them on an irresistible tide of North Sea oil, but they were fed up with being jerked around by Westminster politicians who had ignored them for years on end and only ventured north when their own careers were at stake. If Scotland was to go bankrupt, they would far rather it was their own government that had driven it on to the rocks.

As the campaign reached its final month, Rupert Murdoch stepped into the mix, letting it be known he had held several productive meetings with Alex Salmond, while the Scottish edition of the *Sun*, which he owned, moved from a pro-Unionist stance to sitting more on the fence. For Murdoch this was both a straightforward political calculation – he never liked to end up on the losing side in any argument and, with the Yes campaign gaining support, he wanted to hedge his bets – and a chance to discomfort the Westminster establishment whom he still hadn't forgiven for disowning him after Leveson. Nigel Farage also ventured north, though many Scots from the No campaign begged him to stay at home, as his pro-Unionist message drove many supporters away; whatever side of the debate Farage was on, a lot of Scots instinctively felt they wanted to be on the other one.

The atmosphere in Scotland became ever more febrile. Some No supporters claimed they were being intimidated and threatened by Yes campaigners and there were reports of windows being broken and clashes on the streets. Mostly, though, the atmosphere was just passionate: the issue had totally grabbed the attention of hundreds of thousands of Scots who had previously been completely politically disengaged.

The fever finally reached England just under two weeks before the vote, to be held on 18 September, when an opinion poll in the *Sunday Times* reported that the Yes campaign was marginally ahead for the first time. Westminster pressed the panic button. The break-up of the Union was now a real possibility rather than just a hypothetical scenario and no one knew exactly what the consequences would be or even what precise measures would need to be taken to achieve the separation. All they knew was that it was all bad.

The timing of the poll couldn't have been worse for David Cameron, as it coincided with the prime minister's annual visit to Balmoral to spend the weekend with the Queen. Breakfast on the Sunday morning must have been an awkward affair. The Queen could at least point out that she was doing her bit to save the Union, as the following day the royal family announced that the Duchess of Cambridge was pregnant with her second child. The threat to Scotland was implicit: if you become independent the closest you will ever get to seeing the royal baby will be in the pages of *Hello!* The prime minister couldn't even claim to have watched the first televised debate between Alex Salmond and Alistair Darling as, like almost every other Westminster politician, he hadn't at the time considered it to be very important. It is safe to assume, though, that Cameron left Balmoral with a royal flea in his ear and a reminder of the shame he would feel if he was to be remembered as the prime minister who lost the Union. Even the upside of being able to tell Ukip he had met the government's immigration targets by losing 4.5 million people in a day was little consolation.

On Cameron's return to London, Downing Street let it be known that the prime minister was taking the situation so seriously he wouldn't be returning to Scotland before the referendum. This wasn't quite as contrary as it appeared. Cameron understood how much he personally and the Tories in general were disliked in Scotland: a personal appearance north of the border risked tipping even more of the undecided voters into the Yes camp. Within a day, though, he had re-thought his position. Something must be done. He would be going to Scotland after all – if only to prove that he wasn't ducking the issue and terrified of his own toxicity.

In a rare show of cross-party unity – aka desperation – the three party leaders in Westminster announced there would be no Prime Minister's Questions on Wednesday, 10 September and that instead they would all be flying to Scotland to persuade, beg or bribe the Scots to stay part of the UK. Cameron would be going to Edinburgh, Ed Miliband to Glasgow and Nick Clegg to . . . No one was really very interested where the Lib Dem leader was going, least of all the Scots, but he couldn't very well be left behind. That, though, was his own private tragedy rather than the nation's.

Cameron's trip to Edinburgh had all the hallmarks of late planning. He couldn't be allowed out on the street to meet people in case he was lynched, so he needed a safe space where he was guaranteed a reception that would be, at worst, indifferent. Tory Central Office came up with the headquarters of the financial services company Scottish Widows; it was never made plain whether the Tories were aware that Scottish Widows had for years run a very successful campaign in which a young woman had made no effort to disguise her joy at the death of her partner, or whether this was the best they could come up with at short notice.

For his half-hour in Scotland, the prime minister was

perched on a stool, willing a tear to form. He hadn't come to tell the Scots the hard realities of independence; they had already been told they would be broke hundreds of times already, so there was no need. Instead he was going to talk from the heart about how much he loved them and how sad he would be if they left. He talked of a shared history and of crags and glens. He refrained from getting misty-eyed over the ghillies and beaters he had known as a child when his family had holidayed on the isle of Jura, but his sentiments did frequently seem closer to a nineteenth-century Landseer painting than a twenty-first-century Scotland his audience might recognize. But Cameron was determined to tell it like it was.

'People can feel it's a bit like a general election,' he said, 'that you make a decision and then five years later you can make another decision. If you're fed up with the "effing Tories", give them a kick and maybe we'll think again . . . This is totally different.' The use of 'effing' was intended to show just how passionate Cameron felt about Scotland, but as little the prime minister says – especially on such an important occasion, with media from all over the world present – is unscripted, it sounded more like a posh boy trying to talk to the potty-mouthed Scots in their own language. This suspicion was fuelled by what followed. Having promised to speak from the heart, Cameron spent a great deal of the latter part of his speech talking from the head, reminding the Scots they would have no banks, no money, no jobs and no houses if they left the Union. Their only prospects would be to become like Panama, laundering money for Mexican drug cartels. After their own experience of Fred the Shred Godwin running Royal Bank of Scotland into near bankruptcy, that might have been an attractive prospect to some Scots. As Cameron headed back to England, some observers thought they saw tears in his eyes. Others saw only signs of moisture on his chin.

Although there had been only the one poll putting the Yes vote ahead, the others were far too close for comfort, ranging from 53–47 to 51–49 in favour of staying in the union, so it was all hands to the pump for the No campaign. As more and more traditional Labour voters switched to the Yes side, the amateur nature of Labour's organization became more and more self-evident. At general elections, the Labour vote had often been weighed rather than counted: Labour candidates were so used to winning huge majorities that the local Labour parties had taken their support for granted and had made no effort to find out who had voted for them or to keep a record of their names and addresses. So when the polls started moving against them, Labour had no idea which voters might need more persuasion, nor did they have the means of locating them. It was, as one Westminster Labour MP put it, 'a shambles'.

With time running out and Miliband's Glasgow rally having made few headlines, Labour brought in its biggest gun of all, Gordon Brown, to help save the Union. For Alistair Darling, who had been leading Labour's campaign in Scotland, this was both a humiliation and a nightmare. Darling and Brown had barely spoken to each other since Labour lost the 2010 election; to say they disliked each other would be an understatement. Even while in office, Darling had accused Brown of 'unleashing the forces of hell' on him, and now he was going to have to take a back seat on the platform while Brown unleashed those same forces on Alex

Salmond and be forced to grin and applaud enthusiastically.

Within days of Brown's arrival, the mood changed, even if the opinion polls remained finely balanced. The No campaign became louder and more insistent, calling in everyone from the governor of the Bank of England, the Queen, EU leaders and Barack Obama to Eddie Izzard to lend their support. It wasn't entirely clear what the comedian had to offer. 'I've run six marathons in Scotland,' he told a meeting in Glasgow, while doing a warm-up act for Gordon Brown, 'and I love Scotland, so please don't leave the UK. It would be terribly sad if you did and I want you to be happy.' It was more psychotherapy than a rallying cry, though by now every little helped.

The biggest change in the No campaign came during the final weekend before the referendum when concessions were made to the independence movement:

Brown: It's not working.
Cameron: How do you mean?
Brown: The scare tactics. The Scots don't care. No matter how often we tell them they will be broke, their country boarded up, their half of the submarine scrapped and that they will never see daylight again, they're not bothered. Half of them reckon they are rich, the other half reckon they're poor, but they all reckon they will be better off if they were running the place. And, to be fair, they have a point . . .
Cameron: So what do you reckon?
Brown: We have to throw them a bone. We have to tell them they can have devo max anyway.
Cameron: We can't do that. I deliberately kept it off the ballot paper . . .

Brown: I know. That's not looking such a clever move now.
Cameron: But the right-wingers in the Tory party will start going mad that we're giving away too much and the Ukippers will start demanding independence for Clacton.
Brown: You don't have a choice. If you want to save the Union, the least you can offer is devo max. You can worry about your backbenchers and Ukip when the referendum is over.

Cameron returned to Scotland for a final time on the Monday before the ballot, flying in to Aberdeen to give a speech at the Aberdeen Exhibition and Conference Centre – more usually the venue for talks on job opportunities in the South Korean oil industry and One Direction concerts – to an audience of eight hundred specially bussed in for the occasion. They might have been the entire membership of the Scottish Conservative party. This time there was no effing or blinding, just a repetition of how much he loved Scotland, and how any Scot that got arrested in Magaluf would rot in jail indefinitely as they would not have access to a consular official. The pay-off, though, was devo max. If Scotland stayed it could have anything it wanted. Money. Love. Good looks. Sunshine. Anything but independence. The speech over, Cameron returned to London with his fingers crossed. The last few days of the No campaign were in Labour's hands.

The final push didn't get off to the best of starts. One of the attractions of the Yes campaign had been its engagement with ordinary people: Alex Salmond had been prepared to go out on the streets and talk to people; if necessary, he would win Scotland over postcode by postcode. The leaders of the three Westminster parties had only ever talked at meetings where lobbyists, apparatchiks and the security detail had vetted the audience: this was part habit and – as far as Cameron and Clegg were concerned – part necessity. Miliband was the only Westminster leader who could do a walkabout without provoking too angry a reaction and, to his credit, he arranged one in an Edinburgh shopping mall.

It wasn't entirely Miliband's fault that it went hopelessly wrong, though his back-room team could possibly have foreseen the trouble. The referendum campaign had generated massive interest outside the UK, and film crews and journalists from all over the world – along with the English and Scottish media – were lying in wait for him. He eventually arrived from the opposite direction than had been anticipated and within seconds there was a media stampede and Miliband was surrounded by cameramen and reporters shoving cameras and microphones in his face. The event quickly turned into a piece of political performance art, street theatre created by Miliband and the media almost exclusively for their own benefit.

The walkabout became a rolling maul, with Miliband at the centre and a handful of Yes protestors chanting on the periphery. Realizing he had nearly been carried out of the mall without actually talking to a single voter, the Labour leader made a desperate lunge for the nearest shop. It turned out to be a hairdresser's called Super Cuts. The own goal was complete. Having chatted to a dazed teenager for a few moments, Miliband made for the car park. The staged event had lasted less than five minutes, all of which had been pure chaos.

Elsewhere, Labour was being rather more effective.

Having dozed through the first two years of the campaign, the Scottish Labour party had upped its game and now began to challenge Salmond more directly – particularly on the NHS. This had been a tricky area for Labour, as it too had spent the past few years criticizing the Tories' gradual privatization of the NHS and was now forced into finding a middle ground in which the health services weren't safe in the SNP's hands either. They did it by finding a £450 million hole in the SNP's funding plans for the NHS. The figures were disputed, but a wedge had been created and the fight-back had begun.

It was led by Brown, who went from community centre to community centre, imploring the Scots to remain part of the Union. He saved his best till last, with a speech in the Maryhill district of Glasgow. He cut the jokes – always a blessing – and became his father's son, though he sounded more like a Southern evangelist than a methodist. 'Comrades,' he said. The Tories and the Lib Dems in the audience cheered as loudly at this as the Labour supporters; the No campaign had made strange bedfellows of mortal enemies. What two world wars had brought together, 'let no narrow nationalization split asunder,' he continued. Independence wasn't a progressive form of politics, it was a step backwards. A race to parochialism, a race to the bottom on tax, a race to Conservatism. This was the authentic Gordon Brown that had been kept under wraps while he was prime minister for fear of sounding too radical. If it was his political epitaph, it was a hell of a way to go out. Certainly better than Donald Dewar, the former Labour MP and first-ever first minister of Scotland, whose statue stood at the head of Glasgow's Buchanan Street. For months no one had bothered to remove the pigeon shit from his head; now, to add insult, someone had put a Yes sticker on his jacket lapel.

Over in the Yes camp, Alex Salmond was having problems of his own. Although a long-time member of the Scottish political establishment, he'd built much of his campaign on being the underdog, the outsider Westminster was trying to keep at bay. Once the polls became neck and neck, it was much harder to play the underdog card. With the concession of devo max a week before the referendum, he was already assured of everything he would have settled for three years earlier. It was no longer enough just to set himself up in opposition to the establishment. He managed, with some success, to turn the English media – Nick Robinson and the BBC in particular – into the enemy, but the threats of a 'Day of Reckoning' for Scottish businesses supporting the No campaign had backfired on him and he found it hard to win over the critical last undecided voters, who had no trouble hating the Tories and Westminster but needed convincing that an independent Scotland was a realistic proposition, that Salmond was on top of the practical details of how the new order would work.

If Salmond did know, he kept it to himself. The suspicion was that he had as little idea of the mechanics of separation as Cameron and Miliband; the difference was that for them it wasn't an issue. In his last few speeches, the only answer Salmond had left was to contradict. The No campaign said he was planning to take £450 million from the NHS budget; Salmond just said he wasn't. The No campaign said Scotland wouldn't be able to use the pound; Salmond said it would. And so on. Few details were ever given and during his final rallying cry at Perth on the night before the referendum all he did was to repeat the same message over and over again in a quavering voice reminiscent of Martin Luther King and Barack Obama: 'Yes we can. Yes we can.'

It wasn't enough. When the votes were counted, a Red Sea of No votes had flooded Salmond's promised land, with the 55–45 per cent margin of victory for the No campaign larger than had seemed probable a few days earlier. Curiously, though, for a campaign that had politically engaged a country – there had been an 85 per cent turnout for the referendum – and had energized the whole of the UK, the actual result was one that hadn't been anticipated. As it happened, no one was particularly happy with the result.

The Yes campaigners felt a huge sense of disappointment at having come so close and failed. Salmond looked to have aged ten years overnight and even a judicious touch of make-up could only reduce that to five. He could – indeed most people expected he would – claim a No vote as a partial victory, having won so many concessions on devo max. To everyone's surprise, he resigned as first minister and leader of the SNP. Either the disappointment had been too much for him or he had realized that his deputy, Nicola Sturgeon, was a less divisive personality. The former was the more likely.

Meanwhile, once the relief of not losing had passed, the No campaign were not much more cheerful. The narrowness of their victory meant Scotland could not be fobbed off with just a few more powers. Concessions that had been promised by Westminster in haste now had to be delivered. And quickly. For both the Tories and Labour, this was a huge problem. Many on the right of the Conservative party thought the Scots got far too good a deal from Westminster already, and David Cameron hadn't had time to consult them before promising Scotland more powers. It wasn't going to be easy to keep them happy: they would want some sort of quid pro quo. More devolved powers for England to match those for Scotland. It was, as a few Tory MPs privately acknowledged, 'a clusterfuck'.

It was just as – if not more – problematic for Labour. Their support in Scotland was now seriously in question. Many of their voters had voted Yes and, were they to support the nationalist movement again in the general election, Labour could lose many of its Scottish seats to the SNP. Saving the Union didn't necessarily mean Labour would save its electoral advantage in Scotland. It might just be that Labour would not be able to get a majority in Westminster without forming a coalition with the SNP.

However, even if Labour could hold its Scottish seats, it still wasn't in the clear. Scottish devolution had inevitably put the 'West Lothian Question' (so called because, in 1977, Tam Dalyell, the Labour MP for West Lothian, was the first to raise the matter in parliament) back in the frame. The question was that for years, many in the Tory party had objected to the idea of Scottish MPs being allowed to vote on English matters when English MPs weren't allowed to vote on some Scottish issues. As almost all these Scottish MPs were Labour and the party might depend on them to get its legislative programme through parliament, Labour had never been keen to debate the West Lothian Question too loudly. Now it might have to, as devolving more powers to Scotland would only make the dissenting voices louder.

Ideally, both Cameron and Miliband would have liked to have taken their time to work out a response to these constitutional matters. Years, preferably. But time was something they didn't have. Scotland had been promised a devolution 'road map' by March 2015 and it couldn't be deferred without rocking the already delicate political ecosystem. Most Scots were on red alert for any signs of hesitation from Westminster: were any to be detected, the drumbeats for independence would start again. The irony was that some kind of independence for Scotland was by now almost inevitable at some point: the No vote had been propped up by the over-fifty-five age-group and, as they died off, there would come a day when the Yes campaign could not be denied.

That, though, was some way off in the future. Westminster politics is mostly about dealing with the here and now, and both parties had to come up with some kind of compromise that would appease the Scots and their own supporters in a matter of weeks. It was a situation almost bound to end unhappily for someone.

Chapter 19

Come Together

FOR THE THREE WEEKS OF THE ANNUAL CONFERENCE SEASON that begins in mid-September, the three parties have an unofficial non-aggression pact. It doesn't always hold. In 2007, Gordon Brown made a surprise visit to Afghanistan during the Tory party conference. There again, former Conservative prime minister Ted Heath had set a precedent for this by choosing to visit Saddam Hussein during Margaret Thatcher's last conference as prime minister; there was no love lost between Heath and Thatcher. But generally speaking the pact was binding. For three weeks only, hostilities between the parties would cease to allow each of them to concentrate on team- and morale-building in their own organizations without any outside distractions.

In September 2014, however, it briefly looked as if the armistice had been forgotten. The Labour party conference in Manchester was due to start just two days after the result of the Scottish referendum had come in and both the Tories and Labour were in a state of mild panic. Having promised Scotland any number of greater devolved powers in a bid to ensure a No vote, they now had to find a way of delivering on them quickly. For the Tories, in particular, this was a problem. With Ukip continuing to eat away at its support, the Conservatives needed to appease its right wing, which felt that Scotland had already been promised too much and that England would suffer as a result. The plan that David Cameron came up with was to insist that Scottish devolution should be matched with greater devolved powers to England: answering the West Lothian Question was to be part of the solution. A quid pro quo.

There were some who reckoned that this had always been part of Cameron's far-sighted master plan and that Labour had been out-smarted all along. This was nonsense; Cameron had been making up Scottish policy on the hoof every bit as much as Labour, but there was no doubt that his proposal of 'English votes for English issues' put Ed Miliband on the back foot. With the Tories having only one Scottish MP – and possibly not even one come May 2015 – the matter of not allowing Scottish MPs to vote on English matters was a non-issue: they could afford to take the ideological high ground with no practical come-backs. For Labour it was much more problematic; with its forty Scottish MPs unable to vote on English issues, it might struggle to get some of its legislation through parliament when it was in government.

At the very least, the Scottish referendum had raised some serious constitutional issues at the very time Labour wanted four days away from party-political matters to concentrate on its own triumphalist knees-up. Party conferences are a moment for tribes to come together, to celebrate their successes – imagined or otherwise – and to lay out their vision for the future. Ed Miliband had unexpectedly been made leader at the 2010 party conference, and at the 2012 conference his 'One Nation' speech had – briefly – raised hopes that he might become a charismatic leader. The last conference before an election was especially important. The troops needed to be energized and mobilized, while the undecided voters and the media had to be convinced that the party had a winning formula.

The last thing Labour needed was an outside distraction, but the Tories made sure they got one. The Scottish referendum had changed the terms of political engagement: large numbers of people who had never been particularly interested in politics had become fascinated by Scotland. Politics had become interesting for the first time in years: people were reading and talking about politics. They didn't know or care about old-school gentlemen's agreements about not disrupting each other's party conferences; they saw that important questions had been raised for English politics by the Scottish referendum and they wanted answers now. Any sign of dithering or delay would be interpreted as the usual Westminster bullshit that had turned so many people away from politics in the first place. Labour had to respond.

What Labour proposed in the two days that separated the Scottish referendum and its own conference was quite sensible: an all-party convention to look into constitutional change. Disentangling all the ramifications of giving Scotland more devolved powers would be a painstaking business. Birmingham had a bigger population than Scotland: should it be given equivalent local powers? Many northern cities – Newcastle, Manchester and Liverpool among them – were all pressing for more say in running themselves. But how much? Cornwall also wanted some kind of independence. And that was just England. What about Wales and Northern Ireland? To carve things up fairly would take time, but the promises made during the referendum campaign denied the parties that time. The Tories had stepped in for a quick kill on Labour, reducing English devolution to 'English votes for English issues', even though they knew full well that was merely a populist soundbite. The reality was that devolution would ask much tougher questions of where MPs' voting rights should begin and end. If Scottish MPs should be barred from voting on English issues, should not the same apply to Wales and Northern Ireland? Should only those MPs whose constituencies were directly affected by legislation be allowed to vote? Why let urban MPs vote on rural matters?

On the eve of the Labour party conference, the Tories took the gloves off and happily portrayed the opposition's proposal as a stalling tactic: Labour, they said, was playing for time and hoping eventually to get away with a few cosmetic changes to the system. At which point Labour appeared to panic. Rather than tackle the questions of constitutional change head on at its conference – using the platform as an opportunity to explain all the possible outcomes – it chose to ignore it almost completely. It was as though part of the remit of the security guards on duty at the entrance to the Manchester Central complex was to hunt down all signs of anything Caledonian. 'Are those Argyll socks, sir? I'm afraid you can't come in with those. Can I ask you a few questions, Madam? Have you or your family spent any time thinking about Scotland in the past six months? You have? Then I'm afraid you're going to have to come with me for a two-hour "Land of Hope and Glory" de-Scottification process.'

The immediate effect was to suck the life out of the conference. While there were some more animated meetings in the fringe events, the main hall barely had a pulse. It was as though Labour had allowed itself to be paralysed by events in Scotland. The party had gone into the conference with a five percentage point lead over the Conservatives; the mood should have been confident and buoyant, a final gathering of the Labour grass roots before the election. It felt more as if Labour was six points behind. Downbeat, apologetic even. The main aim of all the speakers seemed to be to say as little as possible that might frighten any voters. The shadow chancellor's speech on the second day was an object lesson in this. Ed Balls's headline message was, 'I know we were a bit rubbish when we were in charge of the economy and I know I should have done a bit more when I was Gordon Brown's economic secretary. But please give me a break. Things were difficult then and I am now an older and wiser man. I have learned my lessons and promise to be much better this time round. You can trust me. Honest.' It may well have been true, but it could have been better put. The Labour delegates didn't leave the conference hall sniffing electoral victory after that.

Balls's speech was a triumph of substance and nuance, though, compared to Ed Miliband's party leader address the following day. At the Conservative conference in 2005 David Cameron gave the speech that won him the leadership of his party. He did it by talking without notes, pacing the stage with no lectern as a barrier, and the audience loved it. Since then, the note-less speech has become the benchmark of a party leader's speech. A sign of political machismo. In previous years it was something that Ed Miliband had pulled off. This time, possibly due to the distractions of Scotland interrupting his preparations, it went badly wrong:

Miliband: Now here's the thing, friends. The other day I visited an A&E department and I met a guy called Colin. And you know what Colin said to me? He said, 'I love the NHS.' And so do I. Sadly, Colin died. You know what happened then? Well let me tell you what happened then. I went to a college where I met an apprentice. Her name was Elizabeth. And Elizabeth is here today. Where are you, Elizabeth? There you are. Stand up, please, Elizabeth. Everyone, give Elizabeth a round of applause for being an apprentice. Under Labour we will have many more apprentices like Elizabeth. Thank you, Elizabeth. You can sit down now.

Let me tell you something else, friends. The other day I was out walking in the park. Primrose Hill, y'know. I was trying to think about what I was going to say in this speech, actually. Now here's the thing. I met two women, Beatrice and Helen. They were actually hoping to meet Benedict Cumberbatch. I'm pausing for laughter now, friends. Please laugh. Anyway I got chattin' to Beatrice and Helen. And you know what they said to me? This is what they said. They said, 'This Tory government is making it hard for us to complete our doctorates on Victorian women's bodies in art.' And that's not the kind of country I want. The kind of country I want is one where Beatrice and Helen can complete their doctorates together. Because they are better together. We are better together. Which is why I am going to increase the minimum wage.

Now here's the thing, friends. I also met a guy on Hampstead Heath. A lovely guy called Gareth. And Gareth said to me, 'Britain is broken.' And I said, 'I hear you, Gareth.' So friends, I make this pledge to you. With your help, I am going to mend Britain. Together we can. Together we are better. Better we are together.

The applause that followed was more sympathetic than heartfelt. Even without the Tony Blair mannerism of dropping consonants to sound more a man of the people, it had sounded more like a pastiche of a leader's speech, with all its not-so-chance encounters with the general public, than a heartfelt plea to the electorate to share his vision. Ironically, by trying to appear spontaneous and talking without notes, he had just managed to sound more contrived and stilted. Colin, Elizabeth, Beatrice, Helen and Gareth were just mental signposts to guide him through his speech rather than people who had made a lasting impression on him.

Worse was to follow as it soon became apparent that in his speech Miliband had forgotten to deliver key sections on the deficit and immigration. The wound was entirely self-inflicted; there had been no need for him to speak without notes and in doing so he had gifted the Tories a field day. They took full advantage, claiming the Labour leader had missed out these issues on purpose because he knew most people in the country would realize his proposals were inadequate. Miliband was left helplessly wrong-footed: he had to look either incompetent or duplicitous. He chose incompetency and the Labour conference ended even further deflated than it had been when it started. The kindest interpretation was that it had been a holding operation: an attempt not to lose core support or frighten away the less committed, rather than to win over any new converts. As it turned out, it didn't even manage that; by the end of the conference several opinion polls were indicating a narrowing of the gap between Labour and the Tories.

There was one small consolation. As the situation in Iraq and Syria had worsened, with ISIS fighters murdering

Western hostages and the US and France having already begun bombing raids in the area, there was pressure for Britain to join in the aerial attacks. This offered an opportunity to deal with the clear and present danger of Ukip, whatever the impact on Isis. After securing cross-party support from Labour and the Lib Dems for raids on Iraq – but not Syria – David Cameron recalled parliament on the Friday, two days after the Labour conference ended, to debate the issue. As the Commons voted overwhelmingly in favour of air strikes, it became depressingly clear that bombing Syria would become inevitable at some stage, that the campaign would drag on for several years and that no one quite knew what eventual victory would even look like other than that 'Iraq and Syria should have stable democratic governments'. Good luck with that.

The Ukip threat to both the Conservatives and Labour was more easily contained, though. Parliament could easily have been recalled on the Thursday, the day after the Labour conference had finished. There was no other parliamentary business scheduled for that day and the Commons more usually met on a Thursday than a Friday. But all three parties checked their diaries, noted that the two-day Ukip party conference was starting on the Friday and agreed that Friday would be much the better day to debate air strikes on Iraq. The party conference non-aggression pact had been called off yet again and the Ukip guns that had gathered at the race course in Ed Miliband's Doncaster constituency had been muted. Nigel Farage's first-day speech received far less media coverage than it otherwise would have done.

Ukip did get its revenge the following day, however, with Mark Reckless, the Conservative MP for Rochester and

Strood, announcing he was joining Ukip. With the Conservative party conference starting in Birmingham the next day – Sunday, 28 September – the timing could hardly have been worse. Just when the Tories wanted to project a united, clear vision for the election, all the focus was on their divisions. The fire-fighting became even more intense late on the Saturday when Brooks Newmark, the minister for civil society, resigned after being caught in a sting by the *Sunday Mirror*. The member for Braintree had brainlessly taken a picture of his erect member peeking through his paisley pyjamas and sent it to the Twitter account of a woman half his age who had been sending him flattering messages. That the account was actually being manipulated by a journalist working for the pro-Tory Guido Fawkes political website only made things worse. Disloyalty and sleaze were not exactly how the Tory high command had envisaged launching the party conference.

Despite these setbacks, the mood in the International Conference Centre in Birmingham was surprisingly bullish throughout the Conservatives' annual get-together. Not even the threats of further Ukip defections seriously spoilt the occasion. (Only one materialized – a former Conservative deputy mayor of London, Richard Barnes, whom no one, not even Boris Johnson, seemed to know.) There were rumblings and grumblings in the corridors and in fringe meetings, but then there always are. Despite being well behind in the polls – Lord Ashcroft, the former deputy chairman of the Conservative party who now ran his own polling company told the Tories on the eve of the conference that Labour was heading for a comfortable majority – the Tories had a swagger and a confidence that suggested they thought they were assured of victory.

It didn't make sense. Labour, well ahead in the polls, had walked around like losers: the Conservatives, their backs to the wall, were totally upbeat. Either both parties were overwhelmed by cognitive dissonance or no one really knew what the hell was going on.

With few people in the halls talking about anything other than the defection of Reckless and Newmark's self-over-exposure, the Tories made a decision to confront the issues head on in the first session. To show they weren't afraid to be open about their local difficulties and could move on. Given Labour's unwillingness even to mention the word 'constitutional reform' the week before, this was a good move. It would have been a better one if the responsibility hadn't been delegated to the party chairman, Grant Shapps, a man so delusional even his mother takes half of what he says with a pinch of salt:

Shapps: I want to address the events of the past twenty-four hours .
Conference: So do we . . .
Shapps: We have been let down by somebody who said one thing and did another. He lied and he lied and he lied.
Conference: That's enough about you. When are you going to get round to talking about Mark Reckless?
Shapps: What do you mean? I am talking about him . . .
Conference: Sorry. Must have missed it. Thought you were talking about your own identity crises when you went around pretending to be Michael Green and Sebastian Fox.
Shapps: That never happened.
Conference: If you say so. Can we move on to No Mark, Newmark? A good knob gag would cheer us up a bit.

Shapps: That never happened either.
Conference: What?
Shapps: Look, read my speech. Can you find anything about Newmark?
Conference: Er . . . no.
Shapps: There you are then. If it's not there, it can't have happened. Would you like to hear my Winston Churchill impressions?
Conference: Have you now changed your name to Bobby Davro? You're about as funny . . .
Shapps: Seriously, I can do it. My mum loves it. 'We will not waver. We will not be blown off course. We will finish the job we started . . .'

At this point even the poor unfortunates who had been lined up on stage behind Shapps, dressed in RAF pale blue T-shirts with large Union Jacks on the front, began to fidget awkwardly.

The first day ended on a marginally more upbeat note with William Hague's final speech to a party conference. He had first spoken in 1977 as a precocious sixteen-year-old who looked about twelve; he was now fifty-three and looked much older. Despite saying all the right things to ensure himself of an affectionate send-off, he didn't seem that sad about going. He still loved the Tory party; the people alongside whom he had to work, not so much.

For his own rallying cry, the chancellor selected Irvine Welsh as his inspiration. 'Choose jobs. Choose enterprise. Choose security. Choose life. Choose good health. I choose something else . . .' Welsh's novel *Trainspotting* perhaps wasn't the most obvious of choices, but it did have a certain resonance. Rapid weight loss, waxy complexion, vacant eyes, a smile that doesn't connect to his facial expression: George Osborne could have been auditioning for the role of Sick George in the film version. His message of austerity was one a dealer might have used to describe a nationwide heroin shortage: 'Labour left us in tough times. They used up the country's entire stash. We have worked hard to get more supplies but there is still not enough to go round. As a result, those of you on benefits will have your maintenance dose frozen at the same level, though due to inflation you will find the actual percentage of pure heroin is decreased year on year. We make no apologies for that, as you should have worked harder. A period of cold turkey won't do you any harm . . . Trust me, I know what I'm talking about.'

This wasn't quite what the party conference had been expecting. It was more usual for governments to announce a series of give-aways at the last gathering before an election and here was Sick George intent on re-branding the Tories as the party of 'Hard Bastards' – an image it had been trying to cast off ever since Theresa May had disowned the 'Nasty Party' associations in 2002. Osborne claimed *force majeure*, arguing that Labour's time in office had left him with no choice – a convenient piece of Shapps-like amnesia that ignored the fact that Osborne's own free-market policies in opposition would have crashed the economy on to the rocks faster than Labour's had – but his positioning was really as much about neutering Ukip as damaging Labour. The Conservatives wanted to stop the haemorrhage of their support to Ukip and being tough was seen as the way forward. It wasn't risk-free: pointing out that the Tories and Ukip were in a battle to clamp down on the poor would also make many Labour voters think twice about joining Ukip.

That, though, was the plan and the home secretary followed up on it the following day. Having begun in a light liberal haze of ending stop-and-search and being nicer to black people, Theresa May turned into Temazepam Treeze. The government was going to give itself powers to lock up anyone it suspected of being involved in undemocratic activity: not just Muslim extremists, but anyone whose activities it didn't like. The tree-huggers had been put on notice. As had David Cameron. Her tough-talking speech had positioned her as a front-runner for the Tory party leadership if the Conservatives didn't get back into government.

Even Boris Johnson caught the mood of conference seriousness. In previous years he had delighted audiences as a comedy turn; this year he was more restrained. He still had by far the best gags, but he was noticeably less of a loose cannon; though not such a team player that he could resist making jokes at Cameron's expense. There were many areas of Cameron's leadership that he might have praised; he chose Europe, the one place where the prime minister was weakest and had little authority, having been out-voted 26–2 during the election for the new president of the European Commission. It was Johnson's way of reminding everyone that he quite fancied being prime minister, too.

Come the final day, Cameron made his own pitch to his party and the country. The plastic podium that had been good for all the other speakers was removed and replaced by Dave's own special, sustainable wooden one, which travels with him everywhere. He walked on to the stage, his hair a little darker than it had been the previous week. That could have been a trick of the light, but almost certainly wasn't.

Cameron: I am a simple man. I walk here before you on my own two feet. Not on your feet but on mine. Because I don't expect anything less of myself than I ask of you. I am not complicated. I want to build a Britain that I can be proud of. That we all can be proud of. It won't be easy. I know that. Standing on your own two feet is never easy. But we can all do it if we try. And I want you to try. I know it's asking a lot, but I want you to trust me.

Trust. That's a very big word. Especially for a simple man. But bear with me for I will deliver on my promises. As an act of pure altruism I saved Scotland for you. And I will tear up the European Charter on Human Rights. Not because it's a populist measure that appeals to the most reactionary members of the Conservative party, but because it's the right thing to do. I am a simple man who only wants to do what's right for you. I know you don't trust politicians. I don't blame you. Many have let you down in the past. So why, I hear you ask, should you trust me? Here's why. I don't take that trust for granted. I know trust has to be earned. So, to earn that trust, here is what I'm going to do. I'm going to bribe you with promises of free money and tax cuts that I will work out how to fund at a later date.

The Tories went home from Birmingham, if not happy, then at least relived and content. Relieved that there had been no new defections to Ukip and content that Cameron's own personal ratings had improved. Scratch beneath the surface and there was a desperate man who would promise almost anything if he thought it would be popular, but on the outside there was a man who was on nodding terms with leadership. Compared to Miliband, Cameron looked like a statesman.

Now it was the turn of the Lib Dems to state their case at

their conference in Glasgow. If Labour had shown it was the party of incompetence and the Tories had shown they were the party of snake-oil, what would the Lib Dems be?

In normal years, the Lib Dems kick off the party conference season; in 2014 they were relegated to the end of the queue because of the Scottish referendum. The timing couldn't have been worse for them. After three weeks of intense activity, everyone – the politicians, media and the public – was all politicized out. It felt as though everything that could possibly be said had already been said. A conference bonus week felt like an unnecessary afterthought. An anti-climax. Precisely the kind of word associations the Lib Dems were fighting to avoid people making with them when they were down to 6 per cent in the polls, neck and neck with the Greens.

The security outside the Scottish Exhibition and Conference Centre in Glasgow was airport tight. Despite this, there were seldom any delays getting in. There were never that many people wanting to attend. All the queues were for a live show of *Still Game* – a Scottish sitcom variant on *Last of the Summer Wine* – at the nearby Hydro. Said it all. The security at the Lib Dems' conference would have been better deployed getting delegates to stay in the complex. There were times when it felt as if the party's delegates were rattling around inside the halls, an ancient lost tribe that was losing more and more of its members by the day as it was airbrushed out of history. A party battling for survival. A party that wasn't even sure what it was it was dying of but had come to Glasgow in search of a miracle cure.

There were none on offer. If an upbeat, revivalist message was what was needed, then Danny Alexander wasn't the man to give it. The chief secretary to the Treasury may have been one of those in the Lib Dem leadership eyeing up Nick Clegg's job, but if he gets it it won't be because of his oratory. Alexander came on stage jacket- and tie-less, with his sleeves rolled up to just above his wrists – steady, Danny – as if to show he meant business and had come out fighting. 'I want you to roll up your sleeves and tell our story,' he said limply, his doe eyes and fallen shoulders suggesting he had already given up.

His trouble was that the story Alexander wanted to tell was one that even he struggled to believe. It was that the Lib Dems had been the beating heart of the government. Without the Lib Dems the road improvements to the A1 and the A303 would never have happened. The Lib Dems had single-handedly rescued the economy and Britain. Not once, but three times. Somehow, though, they had failed to get the credit they deserved for standing up to the Tories. As all that anyone could remember of Alexander during the past four and a half years was of a politician who gave the impression of being more Tory than the Tories, someone who seemed thrilled to be sitting alongside Cameron and Osborne, someone who seldom had a word of criticism for any government economic policy, the audience was understandably confused by this. His only explanation was that he had been suffering from Stockholm syndrome. He had been so brutalized by his captors that he had fallen in love with them. Only now, with just seven months to the election, had he recovered sufficiently to say that the Tories would have been even worse without them.

It was much the same message that Vince Cable had for the conference the following day. Cable put it across with rather more conviction and was rewarded with more generous applause, but he was still fighting to paper over the logical inconsistencies in the Lib Dem cause. It was striking that no speaker at the conference ever used the word 'trust'. At most party conferences 'trust' is a word thrown around as freely as election give-aways. 'Trust us. We're different.' In Glasgow it was on the banned list. Everyone knew that this particular trust fund was now empty. The Lib Dems had asked for trust too many times in the past and had failed to deliver on their promises. Now even the hard-core, most loyal members didn't really trust the party leadership.

It was a problem for everyone. Key speaker after key speaker came up on stage to say how well the party had done in government, without referring to the fact that its support was falling off a cliff face. Key speaker after key speaker came up on stage to make promises – many of them sensible – about what they would do in government, without referring to their previous promises having been rendered largely meaningless. Their three big ideas at the last election – tuition fees, electoral reform and Lords reform – had all died a nasty death early on in government, leaving the Lib Dems little narrative other than that they had made the Tories be a bit less nasty than they otherwise would have been. That may have been true, but it was hardly the most positive of messages on which to campaign; nor did it stop many Lib Dem supporters thinking the party hadn't been nearly as effective in curbing the Conservatives as it should have been.

All of which meant that much of the Lib Dem conference took place in suspended animation. Promises were made and listened to, but no one – not even those making them – had any idea whether they were red-line issues or just another meaningless, feel-good wish-list, as the key determinant of this was also off limits. The Lib Dems knew they were going to take a beating at the next election and would, at best, be left with thirty-two MPs, but they could still form a coalition. The question was with whom and on what terms? No one was prepared to say. This was, apparently, another taboo topic. A few speakers went so far as to say they didn't much like the Labour leadership, but then felt obliged to follow up by saying they didn't much care for Tory policies either, before going on to maintain the illusion that they were fighting the election to win it. It was a way of passing the time, of getting through the conference without too many disagreements, but it wasn't particularly enlightening or rewarding for anyone.

With so little clarity on offer in the main hall, most members headed for the fringe meetings. These events had an energy that was missing elsewhere, even for topics such as 'Dignity in Dying' – a subject particularly close to home this year – and 'Is it possible to be a Christian Humanist?' This being the Lib Dems, the answer was a 'Yes in some cases'. It was exhausting for the party elite, though. Each fringe event required the presence of at least one Lib Dem celeb – someone who inspired name, if not facial, recognition – which meant that MPs such as Julian Huppert were whisked around the conference on a never-ending conveyor belt. It was almost as if the organizers had a deal with a lookalike agency. Yet even on the fringe, the key issue of what the party might look like after the election and what coalition deals might be made were fudged: no one wanted to spoil the fun by staring into the abyss. Instead, many sessions were taken up with a retreat into the core values of the party on issues such as flood defence, bees, Gatwick airport and garden cities. Passions raged much fiercer over whether an amendment to lines 19–20 on one motion should include the words 'and climate change'. That debate went on for more than an hour before it was narrowly thrown out.

All good things come to an end, though. As did the Lib Dem conference. All of Nick Clegg's closing speech had already been leaked and reported on before he made it, so even that came as an anti-climax. There were a few rumours on the morning that Clegg might throw in a surprise and announce his resignation, but these were started more to whip up some interest in the end of the conference than in any belief that it might actually happen. Not even the Lib Dems could self-destruct on such a grand scale.

Having wisely replaced the 'Winning Here' signs on the conference hall wall with the Lib Dems' bird logo, Clegg bounced on stage for the finale and gave it his all for the best part of an hour. It was his best speech for some years, better delivered than many expected, but it still wasn't enough. The disconnect between the passion with which he spoke and the belief he had in what he was saying was all too apparent. Even to Clegg. His eyes had that 'Get me out of here' look right from the start. The fault-lines in the Lib Dems' recent history were just too large to be crossed:

Clegg: We have been at the heart of this government. *We haven't.* We are the only party that can stand up for liberal values and put an end to the simplistic politics of left and right. *If only that were true.* We are the only party that offers a vision of hope. *Why am I sounding so desperate?* Time and again we have stood up to the Tories in coalition. *Though invariably we were rolled over.* We have made sure that early-years education has been at the forefront of this government. *Please don't remember we helped end hundreds of Sure Start programmes.* I know we have made some mistakes in government. I accept that. *I can hardly deny it.* Any party in its first ever term in office would have done so. *Try telling me that any of you would have passed up the chance to be deputy prime minister.* We got it wrong on tuition fees. *We also got it wrong on electoral reform and Lords reform but I don't have time to go into that now.* Next time, though, it will be different. *Why?* We won't be knocked off course again. We will be stronger. *Even though our support is down to seven per cent and we predict we will lose just about half our seats in parliament.* We are the party of fairness. *God, life can be unfair sometimes.* We are the party that will stand up for the poor and the marginalized in society. *Just as well, as we are one of them.* Powerlessness is the enemy of opportunity. *Don't I know it. I've never felt so powerless.* So let's move forward together, stronger than ever before, and lead the country at the next election. *Though almost certainly without me as leader of this party. Stop laughing, Vince, Danny and Tim.* Thank you. *Thank you and good night.*

Clegg left the auditorium to a dutiful ovation that bordered uncomfortably on the polite. For some, the applause was tinged with nostalgia: memories of conferences past at which everything had seemed possible and at which Clegg had unquestionably been the man to lead them to the centre of government. Now the best that was on offer was not to be embarrassed in May and a possible, much reduced, role in a future coalition. The worst was an electoral wipe-out. Either way, Clegg was an outsider to be making the leader's speech at the next party conference in 2015.

So, the conference season ended. Not with a bang, but a whimper.

Chapter 20

Won't Get Fooled Again

THE ONLY CLEAR OUTCOME OF THE THREE PARTY CONFERENCES was that the status quo had been largely kept intact. The Tories had closed the gap on Labour a little – as much due to Ed Miliband's parody of a leader's speech as the conviction of the Conservative message – while the Liberal Democrats still bumped along on 7 per cent, but no party had landed a killer blow on the others. Nor did any party gain a clear advantage in the two by-elections that took place the day after the Lib Dem conference finished. Tory defector Douglas Carswell took Clacton with an even larger majority than expected and gave Ukip its first ever seat in parliament; the Conservatives all but gave up fighting the constituency – Boris Johnson didn't even know the name of the Tory candidate while Labour held off a strong fight from Ukip to hold Heywood and Middleton, which had become vacant after the sudden death of Jim Dobbin a month earlier.

The old hegemony of two-party politics looked as if it was well and truly over. At least for the foreseeable future. No one dared try to predict the result of the November by-election in Rochester and Strood that had been precipitated by the defection of sitting MP Mark Reckless, let alone the outcome of the general election. There was even an outside chance that one, or more, of the party leaders might be replaced before May 2015.

Almost any result was possible. It still seemed likely that Labour would win the most seats – as much due to the fortunes of electoral geography as to the coherence of its message – but nothing could be taken for granted. The extent to which Ukip had made inroads into Labour's traditional white working-class vote in the north of England and how permanent those inroads would be was still unquantifiable. As was the Scottish Labour vote. Many Labour supporters in Scotland had been in favour of independence, were still angry that the party had campaigned so strongly in favour of maintaining the Union and might vote SNP next time. The irony that Labour might have fought so hard to keep the Union and its forty MPs only to lose them anyway escaped no one.

Even if Labour did get the most seats, it was unlikely to have enough to form a majority government. This would mean it would either have to form a coalition or go it alone as a minority government. It wouldn't be a straightforward choice. The most obvious party with whom Labour might form a coalition was the Lib Dems, as they were ideologically closer than any of the other parties. Except there were several problems with this. First was that the Labour and Lib Dem leaderships disliked one another intensely; finding a negotiating team that could remain civil and find common ground might be tough. Labour also might play hardball and demand Nick Clegg's removal as party leader as a blood sacrifice to satisfy it grass-roots supporters, who hated the Lib Dems. Just how much of a sticking point this would be for the Lib Dems was unknown; more of one for Clegg than for Danny Alexander or Tim Farron was as far as anyone was prepared to say.

The trouble didn't end there. The maths of the constituency boundaries meant that Labour would probably poll a smaller percentage of the overall vote than the Conservatives, with the Lib Dems winning a smaller number of overall votes than Ukip despite winning many more seats. This would in effect mean that the second and fourth most popular parties in the country would be forming the government; were they to do so, it would be unprecedented in British political history and there was every likelihood it would be considered undemocratic by many sections of the population. Even with the support of the Lib Dems, though, there was no certainty Labour would be able to form a majority coalition anyway, as the Lib Dem campaign team's most optimistic prediction was that it would win 32 seats. As a deal with either Ukip or the Conservatives was unthinkable and – given the Westminster clamour of 'English Votes for English Laws' following the Scottish referendum – one with the SNP unworkable, the most practical outcome of a Labour victory was that it would go it alone.

Minority government had the attraction of allowing Labour not to have to make compromises with parties it didn't like; nor would it be forced into making promises it couldn't keep. But it was still a minefield. Every new law it tried to initiate would be at risk of defeat; every detail would become a matter of negotiation and the process could grind to a halt, resulting in legislation that satisfied no one. A public already sceptical about the ability of Westminster politicians to tackle the country's problems would become more so and Labour, as the governing party, would get most of the blame. After a year of this, it would be relatively simple for the opposition parties to block Labour at every turn and force a vote of no confidence. At the subsequent general election, Labour would inevitably lose seats.

The Conservatives would be in no more comfortable a position were they to win the most seats but fail to secure an overall majority. As Ukip were predicted to win 10 seats, they were too small a party for the Conservatives to contain and neutralize within a coalition, as they would still not have enough MPs to form a majority, which meant that the Lib Dems would once again be their most likely partner. This would have the advantage of familiarity if not harmony, as the Lib Dems were caught between a rock and a hard place. Without a coalition the Lib Dems would be condemned to political irrelevance for a generation and yet, at a time when its bargaining position and influence was at its weakest with its number of MPs substantially reduced, it would be under pressure from its grass roots not to negotiate away its principles as it had done five years earlier. This would be just as problematic for the Conservatives as for the Lib Dems. With the Lib Dems committed Europhiles and the Tories desperate to avoid losing any more MPs to Ukip, the fault-lines in any coalition were all too predictable. Finding a common ground to keep everyone happy would be almost impossible, and this time round the Lib Dems would be much more likely to walk away from a coalition mid-parliament rather than hang on and watch their support erode still further as they had done last time.

Any coalition the Tories did form would be inherently less stable than the one of five years earlier. Nor would the public be so tolerant of it. The novelty of coalition would have worn off; voters would remember how the Tories and Lib Dems had been at each other's throats in the last year of the previous election campaign and be wary of any reconciliation that appeared to be too conveniently contrived. There was a thin line between political pragmatism and doing anything to grab a share of power, and the electorate was getting much more savvy to it. For all these reasons, the Conservatives' best option might, like Labour's, be to form a minority government. Yet that would come with just the same risks.

There were no easy answers and, in private, some MPs on both sides were thinking that the 2015 election might just be a good one to lose. Let the other side take the inevitable hits and then capitalize on their unpopularity to win an overall majority in 2020. The only two politicians definitely not thinking that way were David Cameron and Ed Miliband, because their jobs depended on the outcome. Only the one who became prime minister would be certain to be still in his job at the next party conference in September 2015; even then, the winner might only be buying himself an extra couple of years.

The closer the election got, the greater became the sense of indecision and paralysis within the main political parties. The opinion polls offered little help or comfort. Within a week of the party conferences ending, one gave Labour a seven point lead over the Conservatives, another put them both neck and neck, and a third indicated that Ukip had the support of 25 per cent of the electorate and was on course to win up to 100 seats in May 2015 – mainly at the expense of the Tories in the south of the UK. It seemed barely credible, but the panic was barely contained as an increasing number of sitting Tory MPs began to wonder if their best chance of re-election was to defect to Ukip. The party leaders had little idea how to calm the nerves of their supporters or what message to give the electorate to head off the Ukip threat:

Cameron: Vote Ukip, get Labour.
Miliband: Vote Ukip, get the Tories.
Farage: Don't vote Conservative, don't vote Labour.
Clegg: Vote Lib Dem, get anyone else.
Cameron: We need to make our message clearer . . .
Miliband: So do we . . .
Cameron: What's yours?
Miliband: That we can actually be quite tough on immigration.
Cameron: How odd. That's ours too. We're also looking at turning the clocks back to 1940.
Miliband: That's not a bad idea.
Farage: You're still getting it all wrong, chaps. The idea is to have no real message at all. I've reversed my policies on the NHS several times and no one either cares or notices. I've no chance of coming up with anything on which disaffected Tories and Labour voters will agree in the long term other than that they dislike things the way they are. All that matters is that I look like an ordinary bloke who drinks in pubs and that I'm not you. You need to be more like me.
Cameron: Vote Ukip.
Miliband: Vote Ukip.
Farage: Vote Ukip.
Clegg: Vote Lib Dem.
Everyone: Don't be silly.

For the British public, though, these were both the most

uncertain and fascinating of times. Would two-party politics be finished for good, or would the old order eventually reassert itself? Would Ukip prove to be a shooting star that burned out, or would it become a permanent part of the political landscape? Would three-party politics become four-party politics? Would Britain remain in the EU? Would Scotland force another independence referendum within a matter of years? What about Wales, Northern Ireland and the large British cities? What powers would they have? The answers to all these questions would ultimately lie with the British public and all the signs were that many people still hadn't made up their minds about what they wanted. Over the next seven months the politicians of all parties would be out selling their ideas and making promises they didn't know if they could keep. Who to believe? The choice is yours. Use it.

John Crace is the *Guardian*'s parliamentary sketch writer and author of the 'Digested Read' columns. He is also author of *Baby Alarm: A Neurotic's Guide to Fatherhood*, *Vertigo: One Football Fan's Fear of Success*, *Harry's Games: Inside the Mind of Harry Redknapp*, *Brideshead Abbreviated: The Digested Read of the Twentieth Century* and *The Digested Twenty-first Century*. He lives in London.